MY
BUSINESS IN
ROMANIA

™

Copyright © 2020 Maria Piroi, Bogdan Nastase

All rights reserved

ISBN-13: 979-858-3695-97-3

The views expressed in this book belong entirely to the authors and do not in any way involve the responsibility of the institutions mentioned.

While every precaution has been taken in the preparation of this book, the authors assume no responsibility for errors or omissions, or for damages resulting from the use of the information contained herein.

No part of this book may be reproduced, or stored in a retrieval system, or transmitted in any form or by any means, electronic, mechanical, photocopying, recording, or otherwise, without express written permission of the authors.

Cover design by: Mirela Grinzeanu

Imprint: Independently published

MARIA PIROI, PHD IN ACCOUNTING
BOGDAN NASTASE, PHD IN MANAGEMENT

MY BUSINESS IN ROMANIA

™

FIRST EDITION

MY BUSINESS IN ROMANIA™

DEDICATION

For Ilan

MY BUSINESS IN ROMANIA™

TABLE OF CONTENTS

ABOUT THE AUTHORS	1
FOREWORD	3
INTRODUCTION	5
RULE 1. I DO MY HOMEWORK	**9**
Why Romania?	10
Is Romania suitable for my business model?	10
Is my business model suitable for Romania?	12
Language differences	13
To start fresh or to buy a company?	14
RULE 2. I UNDERSTAND THE BUSINESS PRINCIPLES	**17**
Choose partners carefully	18
Always have a contract	20
Documents must be in perfect order	21
Documents must be stored securely	22
Pay all taxes on time	23
The company's budget is one thing, my personal budget is another	23
RULE 3. I BECOME FAMILIAR WITH THE PRACTICAL DETAILS	**25**
Means of communication	26
How do I choose my office?	27
I open the company. My first steps with the lawyer	30

I choose the right bank and open the account	39
Should I protect my brand?	47
To which authorities do I report?	48

RULE 4. I GET A GOOD ACCOUNTANT — **53**

How to choose my accountant	54
Notary power of attorney for my outsourced accountant	55
Do I need to have an interpreter?	58
The first steps in the accounting of my business in Romania	58
How do I get the VAT code?	59
Deductible expense or not? 5 examples	64
The first money in the company: to lend my business?	68
The first piece of inventory	68
Online tax calendar	69
When moving office	69

RULE 5. I PUT TOGETHER A GOOD TEAM — **73**

How do I recruit?	74
Hiring the first employee	76
HR documents	80
Using the services of freelancers who have their own company	84
Using the services of a freelancer who has a PFA	86

RULE 6. I OPTIMISE MY TAXES — **89**

How to read a Romanian trial balance: examples	90
Becoming familiar with the tax deadlines	107
High revenue, low profit? I need to try this	108

TABLE OF CONTENTS

Hiring an employee	110
Getting tax benefits for vouchers	110
Subcontracting	110
Deducting sponsorships	111
Real estate owner?	111
Understanding my Annual Financial Statements	112
Converting my Annual Financial Statements to IFRS	125
RULE 7. ONE EYE ON CASH AND THE OTHER ON EQUITY	**127**
Why is equity so important?	127
Withdraw dividends only if needed	132
How do I increase the value of my business?	135
RULE 8. FASTEN SEATBELT	**137**
My first tax inspection	138
Get my tax returns certified	139
High Net Worth Individual? Watch out for this	140
In case of an emergency	142
Shenanigans	143
Lessons learned	144
RULE 9. ATTENTION TO THE MOST COMMON RISKS AND MISTAKES	**145**
Not filing tax returns when the business is new	146
Not purchasing the Inspection Register in 30 days from starting	146
Suspending work at the beginning of a crisis	147
Underestimating the importance of cashflow	147
Too large inventories	148

Forgetting important things	149
Expired office rent contract	149
Expired administrator's mandate	150
Lost correspondence	150
Not filing all tax returns	150
Not revaluing real estate every 3 years	150
Neglecting the 6-months rule	150
Documents not reflecting the reality of the operations	151
Ending up with a tax record	151
Not using the crisis as an opportunity	154
Missing the trend towards digitalisation	154
RULE 10. NEXT IS BEST	**157**
Option 1. I sell my business	158
Option 2. I divide the business	158
Option 3. I close my business	160
AFTERWORD	**163**
ACRONYMS	**165**
BIBLIOGRAPHY	**171**
LEGISLATION	**177**
COMING SOON	**180**

ABOUT THE AUTHORS

Maria is an awarded member of the Romanian accounting and tax advisory bodies and runs a successful company in the field. She has a PhD in accounting, has published abroad and has taken part in international conferences. She has developed a unique business methodology based on the best ways to start a business in Romania, to grow it or to exit successfully.

Bogdan has studied at Harvard Business School and has played a number of key roles in multinational organisations from Western Europe, Central Asia and East Africa. Bogdan has a strong interest in stimulating foreign investment in Romania – and is encouraging the Romanian Diaspora return as Entrepreneurs.

> *"We have created this volume primarily because everybody needs reliable information for their business. We have ourselves started companies and helped develop many other businesses, so we know that this information is often scattered, it must be obtained from multiple sources and it takes away time. For our partners, we have always compressed this complexity, offering them simple solutions for their businesses. Throughout our collaborations, many of the local and foreign businesspeople which have built businesses in Romania have repeated to us that without our help and guidance they would not have succeeded - and have encouraged us to put all our knowledge into a book. We have always told them, smiling, that a book would not be enough. And they always replied, smiling, that they could hardly wait to read them all. Well, this is the first one."*
>
> The authors

MY BUSINESS IN ROMANIA™

FOREWORD

To start a business in post-pandemic Romania? I like the idea, but I am temporarily outside Romania, so I am starting to look for more details online. First impression: frequent and unexpected legislative changes, underdeveloped infrastructure, most documents are in a language I do not quite understand, information is not always up to date, bureaucracy seems intimidating and long waiting times seem to be the norm at all levels...

On the other hand, I have heard good things about the attractive tax rates, the business opportunities, the banking sector and the educated human capital, so I want to give the idea a chance, for when the business environment will return to normal after the crisis.

Or - do I already have a business in Romania that I want to grow? But, even before the pandemic, my business had gone flat and was not growing anymore. I do not understand why; I look for solutions online and cannot find them: although the volume of information is high, I find it difficult to select what is relevant; or, on certain topics, I cannot find what I am looking for.

Or - have I made my decision and want to simply close my business in Romania? I am looking for details on how to do it in the simplest way. I would like to start over, either in a new field or in a new country. To close the business, bureaucracy seems also daunting. My feeling of disorientation amplifies...

MY BUSINESS IN ROMANIA™

◆ ◆ ◆

And here is where this book helps me: full of practical examples, the book is making it easier for me to identify integrated, updated information on how to be successful in business in Romania.

INTRODUCTION

What does it mean to have my own business in Romania? What does it mean to develop it, how do I get the results I planned? How does pandemic influence the business environment?

This book is structured so that I understand some of the most important rules for business success in Romania, especially after the crisis. Many businesses have developed by following the principles revealed in this book - and many painful failures have occurred exactly when even experienced businesspeople have neglected these rules. The format in which I can access all this knowledge is meant to reflect my favourite style of reading or listening: the book is available in print, eBook and audiobook format. It is also available in Romanian and English.

Even before I open a business in Romania, I should use the crisis and post-pandemic period to do my homework in advance, and this book helps me with that. First of all, it gives me a clear structure, from the beginning of a business, going through its development stages, and even going as far as closing the company, if I make that decision; Romania has many advantages, but other countries may be better suited for my business needs.

From the moment when I decide for Romania, it becomes very important to understand the practical details presented in this book: video technology can help me stay safe in my own home during the first long-distance calls with the lawyer, for example, but, for certain documents, I will have to be physically in Romania - for example, the first visit to the notary or the bank.

MY BUSINESS IN ROMANIA™

Choosing a good accountant and tax advisor will be absolutely necessary - and will make the difference between the success or failure of my business in Romania. The same will apply to the choice of team members. Having a good tax advisor, I will be able to optimise taxes, keeping my attention on the two levers that will ensure my business' stability: equity and cash. As additional benefits from reading this book, I will find not only ways to choose a good accountant or a good tax advisor but also practical solutions for tax optimisation. I will find in this book the description of the most common mistakes that some business owners and managers make in Romania, especially under the additional pressure generated by the crisis. Reading about these mistakes should not prevent me from exploring what Romania has to offer: on the contrary, I will be much better prepared for the Romanian business environment, with the lessons learned in advance.

One of the objectives of this book is to mobilise interest in the automation of processes so that there are gains for all involved: beneficiaries, programmers, business analysts, even the tax authorities. The project can then be scaled, including outside Romania. Therefore, throughout the book, I can see a series of variables, constants, optionals, classes, structures, functions, loops, protocols - and foresee a set of rules in pseudo-code. Together, they will be an excellent set of technical specifications for a future business platform that can be easily replicated internationally. In this first volume, I identify the variables that influence the activity of my business in Romania. In the next, updated editions of this book, I will also identify new elements of what constitutes a successful business platform. This platform will have a specific national component, regarding the way of doing business in Romania, including business opportunities at the national level - and an international component, which will allow the globalisation of the solution in any country in the world, including a module on international business opportunities. The list does not aim to be exhaustive but to stimulate the debate in the business fields complementary to accounting and taxation.

INTRODUCTION

```
var myBusinessInRomania: Bool = true
```

This book is also full of relevant examples for business people, for High Net Worth Individuals interested in tax optimisation solutions, for lawyers, consultants, business advisors interested in doing business in Romania, for multinational companies interested in expanding their presence to Romania, as well as for Romanian students interested in opening a business. Regardless of the profile, it is very important that, ever since the beginning, I create the company based on what I can do, on what I can, realistically, achieve. Each of us, when we think and create businesses in this spirit, become interconnected and grow together. What we create, each of us, every day, is reflected in the mirror in society.

The essence is to believe in what I do - and to have a motivated team that will be by my side every day, to turn my business in Romania into a success, both after the pandemic - and during the crisis. Intervals of crisis should not discourage me, but strengthen me instead; someone said, very wisely:

"Under high pressure, coal becomes diamond."

❖ ❖ ❖

MY BUSINESS IN ROMANIA™

For the business environment, the experience of a crisis can be countercyclical and can be like a school: in turbulent times an agile business may actually grow, there is much more attention to costs in general, the number of compromises decreases, the degree of innovation in finding solutions increases, no one is waiting for someone else to come and do miracles: even the creators of the companies find the energy resources to put them back on the waterline, realising that every business is a long-distance ship that needs a brave captain and a team to match.

RULE 1. I DO MY HOMEWORK

Before starting a business in Romania I need to analyse the environment, including the ease of setting up a business, of growing it, of paying taxes and of doing business with foreign companies. By going into detail and understanding the business environment of the country, I will be able to decide if it is suitable for my business model - so that I can optimise taxes as well as possible. If I decide to buy an existing company instead of starting a new company, I also have to do my homework.

MY BUSINESS IN ROMANIA™

```
let business = myBusiness
let country = Romania
```

Why Romania?

In just two words: low taxes.

In fact, taxes in Romania are so low, compared to GDP, that Eurostat has just ranked Romania as the second-best country within the EU to be a taxpayer of, in its latest article on tax revenue statistics, from 29 October 2020. Just 26.8% tax revenue-to-GDP ratio for all cumulated taxes in Romania, compared to the EU average of 41.1%. And, even more, the Romanian tax-to-GDP ratio is actually on a decreasing trend, according to Eurostat. And when I also see that the revenue tax for Romanian companies below EUR 1 million may go as low as 1%, it looks like a clear winner.

> *It looks good, really good. But will it be a good fit for my business idea?*

Is Romania suitable for my business model?

Before I start, I need to see in detail how suitable the Romanian market is for my business: How many companies in the target area have the same object of activity? What is their profit rate? Can I make more profit than the competition?

```
var profit: Int = max()
```

If Romania is not the most suitable for my business interests, I could also think about doing business in another country.

RULE 1. I DO MY HOMEWORK

In this direction, The International Accounting Group, TIAG®, offers me a wide range of business guides from other countries around the world.

If, however, I want to deepen the analysis for Romania as a potential candidate, some sources of official information are useful.

The most recent Annual Report on Foreign Direct Investment (FDI) of the National Bank of Romania (BNR), published on 17 September 2020, allows me to anticipate how things will look like in post-pandemic Romania. In this report, which covers 2019, I can see which are the main countries that invested in Romania before the crisis - and the key areas in which they invested. According to the National Bank of Romania, the total value of net FDI flow in 2019 was almost 2% lower compared to 2018, but the balance of FDI increased in 2019 by almost 9% compared to 2018. Almost a quarter of total FDI came from the Netherlands, with a value almost as high as Germany and Austria combined, which are in second and third place, respectively. The following total investment volumes came from Italy, Cyprus, France, Switzerland, Luxembourg, the United Kingdom and Belgium. More than 40% of the total FDI balance went to industry, mainly manufacturing. The rest went mainly to construction & real estate as well as trade. When I look at net flows, the order is reversed and trade came first, followed by production. In terms of geographical location, in 2019 Bucharest-Ilfov absorbed over 60% of the FDI balance, with each of the other 7 development regions having absorption rates of only one digit.

According to its latest Annual Report, which covers 2019, published on 7 September 2020, BNR states the following:

"Foreign direct investment and inflows to the capital account held a lower share of external imbalance financing, down to 80 percent of total (from about 83 percent in the previous year)".

MY BUSINESS IN ROMANIA™

According to the World Bank, which ranks in a Doing Business Index a number of 190 economies, Romania, before the pandemic, was in position 55. It seemed easier to start a business in Romania: the position has increased from 111 to 91 since the last World Bank report, also because voluntary registration for VAT purposes is less time consuming than mandatory registration. But it has become more difficult to obtain building permits (147th out of 190) and to get connected to electricity (157th out of 190). From the point of view of taxes, Romania has eliminated 5 taxes and contributions paid by the employer but has introduced a new labour insurance contribution for the employer. Romania has maintained its leading position globally in cross-border trade.

The latest scoring grades calculated by the three major rating agencies, Standard & Poor's, Moody's, and Fitch, also provide useful information.

```
var fdi: Int = x
var businessIndex: Int = y
var countryRating: Int = z
```

Is my business model suitable for Romania?

Also, another very important step before starting my business in Romania is the following: I need to analyse in detail my own business model, in order to optimise taxes in the best possible way.

For example, if my business model is in the field of services, then the success of my business will also depend on the people I hire. If I save on wages, I may pay for it later, and, most importantly, I will have to pay with my time to correct mistakes.

As a general background, most companies in Romania start as micro-enterprises.

RULE 1. I DO MY HOMEWORK

```
var microEnterpriseTaxPayer: Bool = true
var profitTaxPayer: Bool = false
```

The micro-enterprise is the name of the category, just as the SME names the category of Small and Medium Enterprises. Micro-enterprises and SMEs fall into the higher category of Limited Liability Companies, abbreviated, in Romanian, SRL, from Societate cu Răspundere Limitată. As soon as a micro-enterprise reaches the EUR 1 000 000 revenue threshold, it has its status changed to a profit-paying company.

```
microEnterpriseTaxPayer.toggle()
profitTaxPayer.toggle()
```

Language differences

To calibrate my business model, I need to know that there are differences between the Tax Agency (=*en*. National Agency for Fiscal Administration, *ro*. Agenția Națională de Administrare Fiscală, ANAF) and the Trade Registry on the criteria they use in classifying companies, so I need clarity in the searches for information I perform, as well as in my discussions with business partners in Romania.

```
let taxAgency = taxAgency.Romania
let tradeRegistry = tradeRegistry.Romania
```

In the category of incorporations - legal entities, the Trade Registry includes: general partnership, limited partnership and private limited company; private limited company debutant (SRL-D); economic interest group (EIG); public limited company and partnership limited by shares; national company; European company holding; European company set up by merger; autonomous administration; credit cooperative organisation;

cooperative company of grade I and grade II; agricultural cooperative of grade I and grade II; European cooperative company; European cooperative set up by merger; European company - branch; branch of a company or EIG with registered office in Romania; branch of an autonomous administration; branch of a cooperative company; branch of a company with a registered office abroad; submission of the shares issue prospectus.

The classification of limited liability companies from the point of view of the Tax Agency, according to the annual revenue, is divided into micro-enterprises, which have less than EUR 1 million in revenue, and profit tax paying companies, which have more than EUR 1 million in revenue - with an exception which I will see later in this book.

```
var limitedLiabilityCompany: Bool = true
```

The starting point is the Companies Law, on the one hand - and the Tax Code, on the other hand.

```
let companiesLaw = companiesLaw.Romania
let taxCode = taxCode.Romania
```

The companies are divided by the Trade Registry according to the share capital. The Tax Agency, instead, divides them according to the turnover. As long as the Tax Agency is the one that collects taxes, it is good to know both classifications.

To start fresh or to buy a company?

Beyond the linguistic differences, there are also differences in content: to launch my own company from scratch or to buy it already launched, with a VAT code already obtained and a good banking and tax record?

RULE 1. I DO MY HOMEWORK

In general, it is better to start fresh, just like building a house. If, however, I prefer to buy a company which is already operating, then it is a good idea to do my homework and ask for a valuation of the company, both in terms of assets and liabilities. This is valid also for shelf-companies. In terms of responsibility for past performance, I would think that the person in charge is the former administrator. But the Tax Agency will not look for the former administrator: it will only issue a tax imposition decision on the name of the company, so I have to be careful which company I buy, because I take it with all the hidden flaws.

```
var taxImpositionDecision: Int = 1
```

◆ ◆ ◆

MY BUSINESS IN ROMANIA™

If I have decided on this country, it is time to see which are the principles of doing business in Romania. These principles remain valid especially in times of crisis, when environmental turbulence creates pressure; I just have to follow my principles - and everything will be fine. The most important of these principles - in the following pages.

RULE 2. I UNDERSTAND THE BUSINESS PRINCIPLES

E specially in turbulent times of crisis, it is good for me to grow my company based on sound principles, from the beginning: the more I want a strong company and the more respect I have for the principles, the more proud I will feel when what I have created will start to work. The following principles apply regardless of the country and economic environment. Even more so, I have to take them into account in times of turbulence and in the specific case of Romania, in order to ensure the frictionless success of my business.

```
let protocols = protocol (Zero, One, Two, Three, Four, Five)
```

These principles refer to the people-documents-taxes triangle.

Choose partners carefully

How can I make sure I have reliable business partners? What are the main things that can offer me the confidence that a potential business partner will be able to fulfil obligations without surprises and their company is stable?

I have to be careful when choosing the companies to do business with in Romania, both clients and suppliers. I must first analyse them, based on several criteria, one of the most important of which is equity.

```
var equity: Int = max()
```

What is the easiest way for me to check on equity? I enter the page of the Ministry of Finance, and, on the right of the page, I have the menu Informații fiscale și bilanțuri (=en. Tax information and Balance Sheets). I type in the Unique Identification Code (=ro. Cod Unic de Identificare, CUI), I enter a validation code, then I am presented with the simplified Balance Sheet of the organisation I am interested in, for 2014. I will have to select the most recent year: at the time of writing (October 2020), the Balance Sheets for 2019 were recently published, after the extension of the initial deadline for submission due to the pandemic. I will look at one of the following 3 scenarios:

Scenario One. If the company's equity is significantly higher than the share capital in the Balance Sheet, and the debts are only short-term, this is a company with which I can move on. With the following point of attention: I

RULE 2: I UNDERSTAND THE BUSINESS PRINCIPLES

cannot go further and do business, however, with a company that has share capital RON 200 and equity RON 400: equity must be at least equal to the value of the contract to be concluded and, moreover, I must find the amount at the position in the Balance Sheet *Cash and cash equivalents*. To be safe, I can look in another place: the form in the Annual Financial Statements called *Disclosure data* contains a line called *Cash available in the bank*; if the value of the contract we are about to sign is close to that, then I can move on. The alternative is to ask the business partner to offer me a letter of bank guarantee.

Scenario Two. If the company's equity is equal to the share capital, there is a possibility that the company may not be able to cope, so I have to be cautious in moving forward.

Scenario Three. If the company's equity is negative, I must seriously reconsider having such a business partner.

```
var shareCapital: Int = max()
```

Other criteria for analysis include shareholders, cashflow, business continuity and VAT code.

For example, when one of my local clients has a cashflow problem and goes into insolvency, the Tax Agency can take the money directly.

To check if a company in Romania is has a VAT code, meaning that it is registered for VAT purposes, I can go to the Tax Agency's webpage, type in the company's CUI, then the Captcha code - and obtain the answer instantly.

One of my most important business partners in Romania will also be my bank - so I have to choose it wisely; as I will see in the following chapters, the choice I make regarding the bank can have an unexpected impact.

```
protocol PrincipleOne {
    func partnersVetted()
}
```

By choosing my partners carefully, I will save time later. I can outsource this kind of analysis so that I can receive simplified advice from a team of experts: green - or red.

Always have a contract

It is essential to have a contract with each customer and supplier. This is a good time to focus on the Civil Code, which details the types of contracts in Romania. The process of preparing contracts allows me to apply the 4-eyes principle, at the same time: for drafting and analysing the contract it is a good idea to use the services of a good lawyer, on a collaboration model based on a subscription of even a few hours per month. The price of this subscription might save me a lot of effort later, when my company's activity becomes more complex, exposing me much more to contractual and legislative challenges. It is also a very good idea to have a similar subscription with a tax advisor, which will analyse each contract for me, in terms of tax consequences, and will be able to report to me the deficiencies in the contract - or certain tax challenges that could even lead to the suspension of the company or directly to bankruptcy.

```
protocol PrincipleTwo {
    func contractExists()
}
```

Together, a lawyer and a tax advisor, even outsourced, can better protect me when negotiating, signing and running contracts.

Documents must be in perfect order

Now that I have chosen my partners and have a contract with each of them, operations begin and documents start to be generated. These are supporting documents for accounting - and it is extremely important to have them well organised.

```
protocol PrincipleThree {
    func documentsOrdered()
}
```

Ideally, I should already use a document management system (DMS), which brings structure and order to documents.

Even without it, though, it is a good idea to get used to the kind of collaborative work promoted by Google Workspace (formerly G Suite) or Microsoft, whereby several team members can work on a document or spreadsheet at the same time, reducing the need to use emails, with all their disadvantages. Additionally, the increasing use of video conferencing simplifies things for me, even when I am abroad.

If I use the outsourced services of a lawyer, accountant or tax consultant, it is a good sign when they also have their own DMS platform.

For example, the accountant can show me in real-time on the platform:

- what documents entered;
- what documents came out;
- registered leave requests;
- and many more.

MY BUSINESS IN ROMANIA™

Documents must be stored securely

Once ordered, documents must be stored securely. Like most companies, my business in Romania will keep two types of documents in archives:

- documents in physical format;
- documents in electronic format.

It is always a good idea to have them in the mirror. If something happens to one storage medium, the other remains.

```
protocol PrincipleFour {
    func documentsSecured()
}
```

For paper versions, when I start to accumulate larger volumes, I can use the services of specialised archiving companies, which keep the documents in controlled environments, anti-humidity and fire-proof. These companies can also digitise documents for me, for a fee.

For documents in electronic format, it is important to have them organised logically & securely - and to apply 2-step authentication. Passwords can be broken quite easily, so it is always a good idea to have a second way to confirm identity: a token, an e-token, a code received via SMS, or biometric authentication, for example. Speaking of SMS, I have to make sure that they will reach my mobile number from abroad when I leave the country. There is a specific example of a Romanian bank that uses SMS in different steps of its e-banking system but cannot send SMS to numbers outside Romania. This, however, is more the exception than the rule: most banking systems are adapted to working with foreigners. Also, my documents must be stored securely - but I also need to access them remotely when travelling outside Romania, so I need them in electronic format too.

RULE 2: I UNDERSTAND THE BUSINESS PRINCIPLES

Pay all taxes on time

I have chosen my partners, I have contracts, I have started the operational flow, the documents reflect the reality of the operations - so I start receiving taxes to pay.

Just like the bank, the Tax Agency also has a rating system where delays in paying taxes are considered an element of risk and may trigger a tax inspection.

When I use the services of an accounting firm who prepares my tax statements and tax payment orders, I need to ask them in advance what is the tax calendar applicable to my firm and how can they share with me each update to this calendar, so that I am never taken by surprise by the frequent changes in the tax legislation.

It would also be great if the accounting firm had an alert system in place, able to trigger automatic notifications to my mobile when deadlines approach.

```
protocol PrincipleFive {
    func taxesPaidOnTime()
}
```

Perhaps the most important principle, which does not require additional detail - and which I must always keep in mind:

The company's budget is one thing, my personal budget is another

MY BUSINESS IN ROMANIA™

```
protocol PrincipleZero {
    func separateThings()
}
```

◆◆◆

Having the principles well set, it is now the right time to see what are the details that can make a difference when launching a business in Romania. The first steps with the lawyer, choosing the right bank, protecting the brand, knowing the institutions to which I have to report - knowing these details is essential.

RULE 3. I BECOME FAMILIAR WITH THE PRACTICAL DETAILS

What is the first thing I should do once I decide to do business in Romania? Talk to a lawyer? Get to the bank? Rent a place? Whom should I call first? By the way, shouldn't I get a local mobile number?

MY BUSINESS IN ROMANIA™

Means of communication

Thanks to the European Roaming Regulation, it is now easier and cheaper to speak internationally, but it remains a good idea to have a local number, in order to demonstrate stronger connections to the country and make locals feel more comfortable. Most smartphones now have the option to incorporate a second SIM card for the extra number, so it will be easy for me. I also have a very good technical reason to do it: at least one local bank operates only with Romanian numbers for authentication and authorisation of transactions on their platform.

So, on my first visit to Romania, it would be a good idea to buy a local number. I can easily buy a SIM with a number from any of the street shops. I will be asked for my ID and to choose between a prepaid card or a subscription. Each of these two options comes with its own advantages and disadvantages. Some telecom operators offer very low rates, such as EUR 5 / month for unlimited calls and unlimited internet. As an advantage, the monthly telephone subscription will be a deductible expense for my business in Romania.

// General information: the National Authority for Administration and Regulation in Communications (ANCOM) administers the prefix of Romania +40 and is the starting point to check the status of the telecommunications operators and their coverage, depending on my area of interest in Romania.

```
var localNumber: Int = +40xxxxxxxxx
```

Once I can communicate easily, I will realise, quite soon, that my business in Romania also needs a registered office.

RULE 3. I BECOME FAMILIAR WITH THE PRACTICAL DETAILS

How do I choose my office?

There is a saying in Romanian, roughly translated in the following way:

"Having to move office twice is like having a fire in your building".

If I like moving, everything is fine: I will change the air. If, however, I like stability - but, on the other hand, my business is dynamic and growing, then, sooner or later, I will have to face a major challenge when the place I have invested in becomes too small.

So, I have to choose my location according to my activity - both at present and in dynamics. I have to think flexibly so that I can adapt the space used to the potential increase in the number of team members, if all goes well. I can start by thinking about the number of employees I anticipate having in a couple of years. But, even so, there will still be variability, so I will have to choose, from the very beginning, between several models: registered office at the law firm; registered office at the accounting firm; a cubicle in an office building; or renting an apartment.

The Trade Registry has recently amended the legislation, and now more companies can have their registered office at the headquarters of an accounting firm also, just like it was possible for law firms to do.

There is also the possibility for me to rent an actual office space in an office building, where I have a cubicle for small meetings and regular office work, while, for larger meetings, I have access to a lounge space: there are multinational companies that offer this type of service, including registered office, virtual office and secretarial support.

MY BUSINESS IN ROMANIA™

I can also rent my own office: an apartment, a villa, etc. - in which to establish my company headquarters - but I will need the consent of my neighbours.

```
var registeredOffice: String = Address
```

I have to do an analysis: in the first months, I do not have an activity yet: how much do I have to pay for rent? Maybe I do not need a permanent office, with employees, if I can run my company alone. I can rather use the money to grow the business. And only after I grow will I increase the comfort of the office.

I must be aware there are companies that rent office space for a small rent, but then charge me a lot with utilities and other fees and commissions.

It is ideal for me to rent a well-defined space - for example, a villa, a house etc. - because there I will be better able to manage my costs for what goes in and what goes out, including for the consumption of utilities, as I deem necessary. This way I will obtain lower costs and larger spaces, where I can, for example, organise an archive, or organise my work better, according to business flows.

If I know the business is small and will stay that way, I do not have to take up a lot of space. If, however, I am confident in the ability of my business to grow quickly, then it would be useful to take the space for what my team will already look like in a year. If I take up too little space, then some of the investments I will have to make in the IT system, network etc. will pull me down when I will have to move - and I will have to start over with wiring, moving contracts, reconnecting etc. - aspects that will take up a lot of my time; this time will be nothing else but an opportunity cost: I could have done business development during this time. I have to make a budget, a plan - and tell myself:

RULE 3. I BECOME FAMILIAR WITH THE PRACTICAL DETAILS

"In x months I want to get to this point, in y months I want to be at that point."

Thus, I will know where to rent, when to invest in facilities, equipment, contracts etc.

If I want my business in Romania to be successful, I have to choose people with experience. And these people will have the expectation of a nice office. Because, otherwise, the lack of experienced people in the team will facilitate problems that I will only be able to solve by redirecting some of my time; but this time I also have to dedicate for business development, not only for operational aspects. So I will have to make, permanently, decisions: what office I choose, what people I choose in the team, in what I invest my main resources: time and money. Otherwise, I will remain, permanently, only with regrets such as *"what would have been, if it had been"*.

But, strictly at an operational level, this is the moment when I have to deal with some practical details. Among them - the actual opening of the company and the obtaining of a VAT code. A lawyer will help me to open the company and the accountant to get the VAT code. It is very important to have a contract for the office: it will be required both for opening the company and for obtaining the VAT code. If I carry out an activity for which it is important to have a VAT code - more on this subject in the next chapter - I must know that the Tax Agency does not register my company as a VAT payer if I do not have a registered office contract for a period of at least one year. When I choose my accounting firm, I can ask them if I can have my registered office with them. Thus, on the one hand, I will get a positive score from the Tax Agency for two reasons: 1) because an accounting firm is handling my accounting and is a member of the Body of Expert Accountants and Certified Accountants in Romania (=*ro.* Corpul Experților Contabili și Contabililor Autorizați din România, CECCAR) and 2) stability with the registered office. Thus, I can get the VAT code easier.

MY BUSINESS IN ROMANIA™

I open the company. My first steps with the lawyer

I already have a lawyer in Romania. Do I need to come to Romania in person to start the business?

The answer is no. Especially during the pandemic, the Trade Registry has become more flexible. Thus, I can go either to a notary in my city outside Romania or to a Romanian embassy or consulate, to prepare the following documents to send to my lawyer in Romania: power of attorney for the lawyer, signature specimen, and power of attorney for the accounting firm - if I already have one, to process everything necessary in relation to the Tax Agency and be able to start uploading my tax returns to its platform. All these documents must be in Romanian.

```
var lawyer: Bool = true
```

It would take about a month, at a normal pace, until I could hire employees in my new business in Romania. By choosing expedited procedures at the Trade Registry, the lawyer could reduce this interval to ~3 weeks. It takes the lawyer about 1 week at the Trade Registry from the moment the lawyer has all the documents from me - so it is up to me how quickly I manage to get the above documents.

What steps will the lawyer take?

Step 1. Checks the availability of a name for my business in Romania

The lawyer can check for me at the Trade Registry, by filling in a form, the availability of my company's name in Romania. The form is called *Application for verification of company name availability and/or reservation*

RULE 3. I BECOME FAMILIAR WITH THE PRACTICAL DETAILS

thereof. I can express three options - and the first one available will be the winning one. According to the Trade Registry, the brand of a limited liability company consists of its own name, to which the name of one or more partners may be added - and will be accompanied by the full written statement "societate cu răspundere limitată" or S.R.L.

```
var companyName: String = ""
```

If I also have a logo, now is a very good time to check if it is available for registration in Romania as well. The form is called *Application for verification of the logo/emblem availability and/or its reservation thereof.*

Step 2. Prepares the documents for me to sign and the rest of the folder

The lawyer will have to prepare the full folder for the Trade Registry on my behalf. This folder includes documents that I have to provide to the lawyer in a copy, for example, identity documents, property titles, account statements - and the set of documents for me to sign. Since I take for granted what someone else has prepared for me, it is a good idea for me to know what each document is about - and to read them carefully. If I do not speak the language, it is good to ask the lawyer for bilingual versions of each of the documents.

The first document that the lawyer offers me pre-filled, for me to sign, is the Registration Application. This is a two-page document, which contains details about me, about the future firm, as well as an outline of the documents that the lawyer must submit on my behalf.

The registration application has a first Annex regarding fiscal registration, in which I declare the main data regarding the tax vector (tax profile) of my business in Romania: profit tax - quarterly / annually - or on the incomes of micro-enterprises; the number of employees, estimated total income.

Also, on a monthly or quarterly basis, where applicable, I have to declare the following: tax on income from salaries and income assimilated to salaries; contribution for social health insurance; unemployment insurance contribution; insurance contribution for work accidents and occupational diseases; social insurance contribution; contribution to the Guarantee Fund for the payment of salary claims; contribution for holidays and allowances.

If I have foreign citizenship and am domiciled outside of Romania, I must complete a second Annex regarding foreign investment, with the value and the associates/shareholders domiciled abroad. As general information, this annex will also be required in case of capital increase or reduction, as well as in case of transfer of shares.

The next document required by the Trade Registry is an affidavit, a statement on my own responsibility that I have not already worked without registration. Also, I need to confirm the following:

> "I undertake that, before starting the activity, I must submit the affidavit regarding the legality of carrying out the activities declared according to the provisions of Law no. 359/2004, with the subsequent changes and completions and, for the activities with significant impact on the environment, to request the authorisation at the headquarters of the public authority for environmental protection".

This affidavit must also show that my business in Romania meets the operating conditions provided by the specific legislation in the field of sanitary, sanitary-veterinary, environmental protection and labour protection.

One of the most important documents that my lawyer prepares for me is represented by the Articles of Association.

RULE 3. I BECOME FAMILIAR WITH THE PRACTICAL DETAILS

```
var articlesOfAssociation: String = ""
```

The forms in which the Articles of Association may take shape include the authentic form, mandatory if there is a plot of land among the goods subscribed as a contribution in kind to the share capital - or other forms, if there is no land among the goods subscribed as a contribution in kind to the share capital. These other forms include: concluding the deed under private signature; attestation by the lawyer, according to the Lawyers' Law; giving a definite date: in front of a public notary or in front of the support service within the Trade Registry.

The Trade Registry offers very useful models of the Articles of Association for limited liability companies with one or more shareholders, templates which includes the following elements: legal form, name, duration of the company, registered office, object of activity, share capital, management, administrator, activity, dissolution and liquidation, litigation and final provisions.

The legal form has the following characteristics: limited liability company; Romanian legal entity; carries out its activity in accordance with Romanian laws; carries out its activity in accordance with the Articles of Association (Statute); the modification of the legal form is made by the decision of the associate; the company is the holder of rights and obligations; the company is liable to third parties with the entire patrimony.

The name of the company receives the suffix *SRL*, and the complete addressing formula includes its name, legal form, registered office, registration number in the Trade Registry, unique registration code and share capital. When I create my website, I have to mention all these above elements. When I want to change the name of the company, I can do it by decision, but only after I have checked the availability of the new name.

The duration of the company can be either unlimited or limited, for a period of x years, from the date of *dd.mm.yyyy* to the date of *dd.mm.yyyy*.

The registered office is the company address - which can be moved. I will be able to set up secondary offices - branches, agencies, representative offices or other units without legal personality - also at other addresses, in other cities from Romania, as well as in other countries.

Regarding the company's object of activity, the key concept is that of CAEN, short for the Classification of Activities in the National Economy. This classification is administered by the National Institute of Statistics - and is aligned with the Nomenclature of Activities in the European Union - NACE. I must indicate a primary CAEN code - and several secondary CAEN codes.

The share capital is subscribed and paid either in cash (in RON or foreign currency) or in-kind - in which case the value must be certified by an expert report - resulting in a number of x shares, with a nominal value of y RON / share. The share capital may be reduced, but only after at least 2 months. It may be increased, in-kind or in cash. It may also be transferred in whole or in part - and the transfer must be registered at the Trade Registry, registered in the register of associates of the company, as well as published in the Official Journal.

The management of the company, according to the Articles of Association, has a strong role related to approving of the Annual Financial Statements, deciding on the distribution of the net benefits, appointing administrators and auditors, and amending the Articles of Association.

The company administrator can either be me or someone else I empower.

The duration of the mandate can either be mentioned in the Articles of Association - or not. If the duration of the mandate is mentioned in the Articles of Association, it can be either unlimited or for a period of x years.

RULE 3. I BECOME FAMILIAR WITH THE PRACTICAL DETAILS

If the duration of the mandate is mentioned in the Articles of Association, then the mandate contract terminates within 3 years from its conclusion, according to the Civil Code.

The responsibility of the administrator covers, according to the Trade Registry template of Articles of Association, the following elements:

"The reality of payments; the real existence of the dividends paid; the existence of the registers required by law and their correct keeping; the exact fulfilment of the decisions of the sole shareholder; the strict fulfilment of the duties that the law and the Articles of Association impose".

The Articles of Association also regulate the company's activity: its financial year (usually from 1 January 1 to 31 December), the need to draw up a Balance Sheet (a condition for establishing dividends), to appoint a censor and a financial auditor.

The Articles of Association offer details about the dissolution conditions, as well as about the dissolution and liquidation procedure. Also present are the litigation details, whether contractual or salary-related.

The final provisions of the Articles of Association link to the applicable legislation:

- Civil Code;
- Labour Code;
- Company Law.

The Trade Registry then requests a Statement on my own responsibility that I meet the legal conditions for holding the quality of founder - administrator - and also provides a template.

MY BUSINESS IN ROMANIA™

Before the crisis, I could have offered this statement either in front of a public notary, either in the form certified by a lawyer, or with a definite date certified by the Trade Registry.

During the crisis, the Trade Registry has made things easier; I can now offer this statement in several ways: registered under private signature, in electronic form, or in the authentic form - certified by a lawyer or at the Trade Registry.

When I have foreign citizenship - or when I am a representative of a foreign legal entity that is not fiscally registered in Romania - I have to offer another statement, which, if I did not already write in Romanian, must be translated and notarised - confirming that I do not have a tax record and that I am not fiscally registered in Romania.

During the crisis, to make things easier, I can offer this statement in several ways: registered under private signature or in electronic form (transmissible by the lawyer to the Trade Registry by electronic means, with an electronic signature or by courier) - or in the authentic form (certified by a lawyer, or at the Trade Registry).

When I choose to be a shareholder in my Romanian company, not directly, as an individual, but through a company from another country, I must present to the Trade Registry a certificate of creditworthiness for my other company, from abroad, a certificate issued by a bank or the chamber of commerce. In this case, I must also submit the Beneficial Owner Form, so that the Trade Registry knows who is actually in control.

Apart from the documents that I have to sign, which the lawyer prepares for me, the Trade Registry also requires a series of proofing documents. For example, a document certifying *"the right to use the space for a registered office, document registered with the fiscal body within the National Agency for Fiscal Administration in whose constituency the building for the*

RULE 3. I BECOME FAMILIAR WITH THE PRACTICAL DETAILS

registered office is located". This document can take various forms: land book extract; sale contract; donation contract; certificate of inheritance; notarial deed of leaving the indivision or delimitation of the property; final court decision regarding the right of property or of use/usufruct; final court decision to leave the division; construction reception report; deed of adjudication of the real estate sold within the forced execution; exchange contract; rental contract; sublease contract; concession contract; real estate leasing contract; loan agreement; contract of use; usufruct contract; agricultural certificate; any other legal act that confers the right of use.

The Trade Registry also requires proof that I have deposited the share capital, either in cash (payment order; cheque receipt) or in-kind: property title (invoices; property titles over the real estate, including the certificate ascertaining the levies on these goods) or the valuation report of the goods. Of course, I must also present a copy of my ID.

Before the crisis, I could have offered my signature specimen either in front of the Director of the Trade Registry or in front of a public notary. During the crisis, to make things easier, I can offer it in several ways, on a template provided by the Trade Registry: legalised by a public notary; certified by a lawyer; in the form of a document under private signature, without any other formality; or, of course, at the Trade Registry.

If I do not perform work at my company's registered office, I must provide a statement on my own responsibility in this regard. If, however, I do, then I must seek the approval of my neighbours and submit documents to the Trade Registry in this regard.

The rest of the folder that the lawyer is preparing for me also includes a series of other documents, such as proof of having checked on the company's name availability and reservation, in original - and, if applicable, the agreement to use the original name.

MY BUSINESS IN ROMANIA™

Finally, I must also present proof of payment of the publication fee in the Official Journal, ~EUR 25 / page. I can make the payment in several ways, including the classic one, in cash at the Trade Registry, or through a postal order or electronic payment order; the list of accounts in RON, EUR and USD is presented on the Trade Registry webpage. If I wish to receive the registration documents by post, instead of having them picked up by the lawyer for me, I can do so in exchange for a fee of ~EUR 2.

Step 3. Registers the company at the Trade Registry

The lawyer goes to the Trade Registry with the documents I provided and submits them. Alternatively, taking into account the effects of the pandemic on the functioning of public institutions, the lawyer may submit the documents by electronic means, by electronic signature or by courier.

Step 4. Obtains my company's Registration Certificate and Registration Resolution

If there are no problems with the documents, the Trade Registry admits the application for registration, authorises the incorporation and registers of my new company, thus confirming the official birth of my business in Romania.

```
let registrationCertificate = registrationCertificate.myBusinessInRomania
let taxIDNumber: Int = xxxxxxxx
```

Step 5. I take over

The lawyer takes the Resolution from the Trade Registry, together with the supporting documents, including the Registration Certificate, and offers them to me. It is now the time to think about choosing an accountant - and to pay a visit to the bank.

RULE 3. I BECOME FAMILIAR WITH THE PRACTICAL DETAILS

I choose the right bank and open the account

Choosing the right bank for my business in Romania will greatly help me, simplifying my money transfers.

What to do before opening a bank account

Before I rush to open an account, it is a good idea to make a preliminary analysis: I may look on the webpage of the National Bank of Romania to see which are the most suitable banks for what I am looking for.

I may also analyse which of the banks are best integrated with international financing facilities, for example with the European Investment Bank or the European Bank for Reconstruction and Development, because these facilities will be positively reflected in more attractive interest rates for me from my preferred bank of choice.

Based on the preliminary analysis, I make a shortlist with my favourite banks. Then I ask each bank in the shortlist for their list fees, commissions and interest rates so that I can compare them. When I tell each bank that I am doing a compared analysis of the facilities offered by other banks, in order to be able to make a suitable decision for my company in Romania for years to come, this should motivate each bank to present me what they have the best and to convince me to become their customer.

The types of packages are named differently, depending on the creativity of the Marketing Department of the bank at that moment: Standard or Premium, Silver or Gold; irrespectively of how they are called, I need to understand the structure of that package and apply it to the dynamics of my company in Romania.

For example, one question I may ask is *how long it will take* from the moment when my company's activity is hypothetically reduced to 0, until someone in the bank would advise me that the Platinum package, for which I continue paying tens or hundreds of euro a month, is no longer suitable for me - and that it would be more convenient for me, temporarily, to switch to a Basic package, which would allow me to optimise costs. If the answer is *"immediately"*, it means that I am in good hands and will benefit from human attention and quality support. If, however, the answer is anything else, including a raising of shoulders, then there is a good chance that I am just a piece in a mechanism, without too much flexibility - and it is a signal that I am in the wrong place, discussing at the wrong table. Rigidity in mechanisms and procedures will not help me when, for example, a new crisis will require quick solutions to liquidity problems. I may be surprised to discover, after a year in which the activity of my Romanian company has temporarily been very low, that I paid without noticing tens or hundreds of euro per month for a premium package which I did not actually use - and no one in that bank noticed or thought that maybe I do not really need that premium package.

The discussion with the preferred banks may start from the moment of depositing the share capital necessary to set up the company at the Trade Registry.

> *"Do you usually finance this type of activity that I carry out? Are you open to funding me in the future if I need it? If so, what would be the conditions? Can we do a simulation on a series of virtual data, just to get a first idea of what our collaboration might look like? This is, in short, the business plan... And if we are to analyse the deposits, what is your policy in this field, how can I benefit from the best conditions?"*

This way, I will see the degree of openness of that bank to working together not only as a custodian of my current accounts but also as a financial arm of

RULE 3. I BECOME FAMILIAR WITH THE PRACTICAL DETAILS

my activities, either lending or depositing. My business will start producing and, in the first years, the commissions that I will pay to the bank for the use of current accounts will feed into its profits. So I may consider it natural for the bank to return the favour when I have accumulated higher amounts that I want to deposit; but it is good to ask about it, from the beginning, otherwise, I may be surprised to discover, after years of collaboration, when I want to open the first deposit, that the bank offers me an insignificant interest, forcing me to transfer the money to another bank, where I will be able to benefit from more advantageous conditions - but where I will have to accept the direct costs of the transfer, as well as the indirect costs of resetting the scoring, grading and rating system.

Here is what a checklist might look like for the first discussion with any of my favourite banks:

Questions regarding account opening

How long does it take? What is the procedure for foreign citizens? What documents are required? Can I open another account remotely or do I need to be physically present? What is the nearest branch? What are the fees for accounts and foreign exchange transactions?

Questions regarding account operation

Does the bank offer *two-step authentication* via an app, or SMS, or token? I have to make sure that the bank's SMS will arrive on my mobile with a foreign number when I leave Romania. Especially in the pandemic and post-pandemic period, when the freedom of movement is affected. What happens if I forget my password? How long can I keep my account open if I do not have transactions? Can the bank offer me a double signature system, in which the accountant prepares my payment orders on the bank's platform, and I just log in and sign them electronically?

Fees for current transactions: I issue invoices and receive money from clients in my bank account; what are the bank's conditions, commissions and fees for this type of transactions? I pay taxes and utilities; what are the bank's conditions, commissions and fees for this type of transactions?

Loans: at some point, I might need a loan to continue my activity: what are the conditions of the bank? Not only the interest but also the rest of the conditions.

Overdraft: how can I get it and what is the maximum value? What are the conditions of the bank?

Deposits: at some point, I will have a surplus and I want to place it in a deposit; what are the conditions of the bank? Not only the interest but also the rest of the conditions.

Questions regarding closing the account

What are the closing fees? How long does it take?

Then I make a table, in which the lines above represent the lines in the table (Question 1, Question 2, Question 3 etc.) - and each column is for each of the banks I go to talk to (Bank 1, Bank 2, Bank 3 etc.). This way, at a glance, it will be easier for me to compare them.

In addition, I have to look at the *ranking of banks in terms of equity*. A good starting point in this regard is the National Bank of Romania's webpage, which displays these rankings. The higher the equity, the higher its stability and its willingness to invest in my business in Romania.

For example, if the bank offers me the opportunity to create high-interest deposits, it is a good indicator that I can keep my money safe at that bank, even adding value. However, at the moment, there are several banks that

RULE 3. I BECOME FAMILIAR WITH THE PRACTICAL DETAILS

offer very low interest rates on deposits: one dollar a month interest, at a deposit of, say, EUR 20 000, is not a very motivating interest rate.
And this is a good time to ask myself:

If this bank has the habit of offering me high-interest loans and low-interest deposits, why am I still here?

All these questions, from this entire checklist, can be placed in a questionnaire, and before I open my account at any of the banks, I may take the questionnaire with me and take the opportunity to ask them, so that I can compare. After filling in the questionnaire, for each of the banks there will be a score - and then, depending on the score, I will know if it is worth considering opening an account at a certain bank or not.

Apart from the objective, quantifiable part, also important is the subjective part: how well received I feel by the representatives of that bank - and at what hierarchical level. I need to have a stable point of contact that I can call at any time without having to repeat the context several times. To which I can go at any time - by appointment, of course - without having to stand in line. A person who, at the same time, is fully prepared to assist me remotely. Especially during a pandemic, it can be frustrating to sit for hours at the entrance to the bank just to enter for a minor transaction, so it is more than useful - even necessary - to confirm that the bank operations of my business in Romania will continue to be fully operational also at a distance, when either I or they will be remote. In addition, I need to see how easy it is to interact remotely with that bank: does it have easy-to-use applications, or does it all come down to email? How many clicks do I have to perform in their application to reach the desired result? For a single transaction, an extra minute may not matter, but when I multiply this by all transactions in a year, I may realise that I am wasting a lot of time with one bank, while another can help me gain time.

```
var bankSelectionCriteria: Bool?
```

The difference is also made by the position from which I go to talk to each of the banks, from the point of view of my own assets, as an individual - and the level in the bank hierarchy at which I am received for a discussion. If I belong to the category of so-called High-Net-Worth Individuals, the degree of openness that I will benefit from the bank for my business in Romania will be higher. However, I will have to be open, in my turn, to explain the source of the money: AML/CFT regulations are becoming more stringent.

By the way, I am not restricted to having just one bank account for my business in Romania: I might be better off with having more. Depending on various criteria - for example, which bank most of my clients already have accounts with, or which other bank offers better interest rates - I can choose to open accounts at several banks. I will do it, anyway, when I open an account with the Treasury to facilitate tax payment transactions. Lesson learned: I need to think wide: I can have an account with at least 2 banks in the country where I go to do business. It is not good to depend on a single factor. Especially since there are times when the banking applications of one or the other of the banks will simply no longer work. Low risk, but with serious impact. Business continuity can suffer: I may end up not paying my suppliers on time, affecting my rating and recording penalties, or I may end up not paying salaries on time - and I will certainly have to compensate for the bank's problems with my own time: instead of making transactions through the bank's mobile app, I will have to go to the nearest branch, which will cost me time, especially if I have to wait for pandemic-specific security measures. And if I am out of the country, it becomes practically impossible. To minimise the impact of such a situation, I need to have a discussion in advance with each of these banks, adding to the initial discussion list, in which to get answers to at least the following questions:

> "Apart from planned maintenance checks, which are always announced in advance, what is the longest period in which your mobile application has not been operational in the last year?

RULE 3. I BECOME FAMILIAR WITH THE PRACTICAL DETAILS

Considering that my business depends on the proper functioning of your application, what do we do when I end up paying interest and penalty fees because the bank application does not work - and I cannot get to your branch either?"

Expectations are that the minimum level of uptime services of the bank application will be 99.99%. So, if the answer is more than 4 hours a month, it is good to think about alternatives. Thus, redundancy is not always a bad thing, and business continuity must always come first.

Account opening

The account can be opened in a few hours. At this stage, I do not have to come to the bank in person. I can empower a representative, who can be, for example, from the accounting firm; the delegate will open the bank account in my name for the deposit of the share capital.

IBAN

Opening an account takes place the same day as going to the bank: the IBAN (International Bank Account Number) is obtained on the spot and is communicated to me.

It is also a good idea for me to ask for the bank identification code, called SWIFT or BIC: it is then useful to include it in all invoices I issue to customers outside Romania: if they pay the invoice only by mentioning the IBAN code and without mentioning SWIFT code, they will end up paying extra fees - and I want to protect them from this inconvenience, especially since it is very simple for me to get this SWIFT / BIC code. I just need to know about its existence, to ask about it, and it will be very easy for the representatives of my new bank in Romania to offer it to me.

MY BUSINESS IN ROMANIA™

```
var iban: String = "ROxxxxxxxxxxxxxxxxxxxx"
var swift: String = "xxxxxxxx"
```

Tokens

It depends on which bank I choose, or, more precisely, if I have a preference for a physical token or an e-token.

The e-token eliminates the need for a physical one, replacing it with a randomly generated code in a mobile application or sent via SMS to a mobile number, to be used as a second authentication factor, in addition to username and password.

A number of banks in Romanian still use physical tokens, while others use e-tokens. A physical token arrives at an address in Romania in a maximum of 7 days. Plus a few extra days if I prefer the bank to send it to me directly to a foreign address. an e-token is configurable from the bank's server and can be obtained much faster: either on the same day or on the next business day.

I can ask for multiple tokens remotely. I do not have to go to the bank.

```
var token: Bool = true
```

Once I have configured all the details regarding the collaboration with the bank, it is good to make a prudent investment in protecting my brand, being careful towards the still unexplored competitive environment in Romania: I invested a lot of time in finding the perfect internet domain, I invested in a designer who created a logo for me that I feel represents my business very well, it would be a shame to discover everything cloned elsewhere.

RULE 3. I BECOME FAMILIAR WITH THE PRACTICAL DETAILS

Should I protect my brand?

Definitely yes. For only a few hundred euro, the benefits of protecting my brand are many. When the name of my company in Romania - or of my main product or service - is a registered trademark, I can develop a set of promotional tools to ensure my recognition, thus helping me to increase sales. Also, the ® trademark symbol will give more confidence to my business partners in Romania.

The process of protecting my brand starts with a query of the database of the European Union Intellectual Property Office (EUIPO), accessible through the TMView tool - European Trademark and Design Network.

```
var tradeMark: Bool?
```

A visit to the website of the State Office for Inventions and Trademarks of Romania (=ro. Oficiul de Stat pentru Invenții și Mărci din România, OSIM) will also help me: the website is generous in information on the steps for registering a trademark, the categories to choose to obtain protection, including an online calculator for finding out immediately the applicable fees.

The whole procedure takes several months, to allow third parties to express their opposition, if necessary. In the end, I receive a certificate confirming the fact that my brand is protected in Romania.

At the same time, I need to start preparing to report my activities to a set of public institutions. Carrying out my business in Romania will also involve forms, specific to my field of activity, so it is good to know already which are the main entities with a role in reporting.

MY BUSINESS IN ROMANIA™

To which authorities do I report?

Depending on the specific type of activity of my business in Romania, in addition to the reports to the Tax Agency, there may be a need to report, one-time or regularly, to other public institutions as well.

Trade Registry

The AML/CFT Law number 129 of 11 July 2019 for the prevention and combating of money laundering and terrorist financing introduced the obligation for all Romanian companies to fill in the Beneficial Owner Form at the Trade Registry. The fine for non-compliance was from RON 5 000 to RON 10 000.

```
var beneficialOwnerForm: Bool = true
```

Initially, this form had to be submitted within a maximum of 12 months from the entry into force of Law 129/2019, until July 2020 respectively. With the pandemic, the deadline was postponed.

Afterwards, on the agenda of the Chamber of Deputies' meeting of 9-10 June 2020 was also the Draft Law Pl-x 297/2020 for the simplification of the procedure for declaring the beneficial owner of some legal entities: in the form adopted by the Parliament, the obligation to submit the Beneficial Owner Form to the Trade Registry was eliminated for legal entities that have only private individuals as shareholders - and remained only for legal entities that have other legal entities as shareholders. The draft law was promulgated by the Decree of the President of Romania number 362/2020 and became Law number 108/2020. The Government Emergency Ordinance 191 of 30 October 2020 has further extended the deadline to 3 months after the end of the Alert Status.

RULE 3. I BECOME FAMILIAR WITH THE PRACTICAL DETAILS

AML/CFT Office

Before I put money in the company, in the form of a shareholder loan, I have to appoint a person from the company to be the point of contact with the National Office for the Prevention and Combating of Money Laundering (=*ro*. Oficiul Național de Prevenire și Combatere a Spălării Banilor, ONPCSB).

I will have to notify the ONPCSB using a specific template available on their website.

The obligation to designate a person as the focal point applies for any amount of the shareholder loan, even, for example, EUR 100.

```
let amlOffice = amlOffice.Romania
```

When organisations need to ensure a corresponding level of compliance with the ONPCSB requirements, it is useful to have the following details at hand about their clients who are legal entities:

> *name; legal form and structure; KYC form; the number, series and date of the registration certificate from the Trade Registry, or equivalent; Trade Registry statement, up-to-date; subscribed and paid-in share capital; tax ID code or its equivalent for foreign entities; credit institution and IBAN code; the list of persons with the right of signature, of the administrators, of the persons with management positions or with a mandate to represent the client - and their signature specimen; the full address of the registered office/ headquarters or, as the case may be, of the branch; shareholder structure; telephone, fax and, as the case may be, email, website; purpose and nature of operations; the name of the beneficial owner.*

MY BUSINESS IN ROMANIA™

INTRASTAT

According to the National Institute of Statistics (=ro. Institutul Național de Statistică, INS),

> "INTRASTAT is the name of the system for collecting statistical data on trade in goods between European Union countries. [...] The obligation to provide data for the Intrastat statistical system rests with economic operators who meet the following conditions: a) are registered for value-added tax purposes (they have a tax ID code); b) exchange goods with other member states of the European Union; c) the total annual value of the exchanges of goods for each of the two flows, inbound and outbound, respectively, exceeds the level of the Intrastat value thresholds established for each year. Intrastat value thresholds represent floor levels of intra-Community trade below which economic operators are exempt from submitting the INTRASTAT statement. Intrastat value thresholds are set separately for each flow and may have different values for intra-Community introductions and shipments of goods, respectively. The information regarding the INTRASTAT value thresholds is published annually, in the Official Journal of Romania, at the end of the year preceding the one for which the value thresholds are in force." (Source: www.intrastat.ro)

```
let intrastat = intrastat.Romania
```

The INTRASTAT value thresholds for 2021 have remained the same as for 2020: RON 900 000 for inbound and RON 900 000 for outbound.

The economic operators providing INTRASTAT data must send to the INS, monthly, until the 15th of the month for the previous month, in electronic format, a statistical statement.

RULE 3. I BECOME FAMILIAR WITH THE PRACTICAL DETAILS

Environment Fund Administration

When dealing with packaging, the online submission of statements for the Environment Fund Administration became mandatory from 2020.

```
let environmentAgency = environmentAgency.Romania
```

How do I submit online statements for the Environment Fund Administration?

The simplest way is through a delegate. In this case, a notary statement is required, to empower the delegate who will represent me in the relationship with the Environment Fund Administration. This notary statement must include the following elements: the identification data of my business in Romania; my identification data, as legal representative; the identification data of my delegate; the e-mail address for notifications, documents and other information issued by the Environment Fund Administration; agreement on receiving information by email; acceptance of the terms and conditions for the use of the Online Statement Submission service.

In the notary statement, I can express my agreement regarding the option to be able to receive documents from the Environment Fund Administration (administrative and tax documents; enforcement documents; other documents) in electronic form - as well as regarding the option to be able to upload documents online, according to the Tax Procedure Code.

If, however, I prefer to submit my statements on my own, without a delegate, I must first submit a request to open an online account service and an application for enrolment, then submit all statements online, according to the instructions in the Guide on how to use the Online Statement Submission service.

MY BUSINESS IN ROMANIA™

◆ ◆ ◆

I will be relieved to discover that, for a considerable number of these reports, a good accountant can be of great help, by taking over some of the administrative tasks from my shoulders and offering me the time I need to deal with growing my business. But how and where to find this accountant? What selection criteria should I use?

RULE 4. I GET A GOOD ACCOUNTANT

"Accounting is the language of business."

Warren Buffett

As soon as I launch the company, some important deadlines start to run. So it is the right time to decide on some important details regarding the accounting of my business in Romania: do I hire an accountant or do I outsource to an accounting firm? Once the decision is made, my accountant will answer some key questions: should I certify my tax returns or not? What expenses are deductible?

How to choose my accountant

I can either hire a full-time accountant or outsource accounting services to a specialised accounting firm. If I find an accountant who works for me as an employee, it is great, especially if the accountant comes with recommendations. Having an internal accountant will be a valuable help, easily accessible, in organising and running my business in Romania. But it will result in higher costs in the beginning, so an alternative is to look towards outsourcing the accounting services to a specialised firm.

```
var accountant: Bool?
var accountingFirm: Bool?
```

There are a number of benefits from me outsourcing to an accounting firm instead of hiring an in-house accountant. For instance, I would usually pay less for an accounting firm than I would for a full-time accountant. A team of accountants deals with more than one business model. Thus, the team of accountants gains more expertise and can be a better solution to assist me with my business needs.

Besides, when I have a service contract with an accounting firm that is a member of professional bodies, I increase the trust of tax inspectors in my company, so I am less likely to be the subject of a tax inspection for the first few years. Professional bodies in Romania are The Romanian Chamber of Tax Advisors (CCF), The Body of Expert and Licensed Accountants in Romania (CECCAR), The Romanian Chamber of Financial Auditors (CAFR), and The Romanian Authority for Public Supervision of the Statutory Audit Activity (ASPAAS).

Ideally, I would like my accounting firm to be ISO 9001 & ISO 27001 certified, for quality management and information security.

RULE 4. I GET A GOOD ACCOUNTANT

Especially at times of crisis, these standards become super useful because they include elements such as business continuity, disaster recovery plans etc. - and minimise the likelihood of scenarios in which the chartered accountant, working from a location other than the office, cannot help me lacking access to documents for technical reasons.

```
enum professionalBodies {
    case aspaas, cafr, ccf, ceccar
}
```

Whether I choose an in-house accountant or an outsourced accounting firm, when they prepare my tax returns and tax payment orders, I must ask them in advance what is the tax schedule applicable to my company and how they will keep me informed of any updates of the tax calendar, so that I am never taken by surprise by the frequent legislative changes.

it would also be great if either the accountant or the accounting firm has an alert system capable of sending me notifications on my mobile as the deadlines approach. I need a tool to help me keep track of various things that may expire and, especially when it comes to the accounting of my business in Romania, such a system will be very beneficial to me.

Notary power of attorney for my outsourced accountant

If I have already decided on an accounting firm to represent me, then a visit to the notary is required. This visit allows me to obtain a power of attorney for the accounting firm, which can then represent me in front of public institutions, including the Tax Agency, and submit my tax returns in the Virtual Private Space (SPV), the Tax Agency's platform. SPV is a free interface that the Tax Agency offers to Romanian taxpayers.

MY BUSINESS IN ROMANIA™

Based on the power of attorney that I offer, the accounting firm can authenticate in my place and upload tax returns or download all the tax-related documents that are addressed to me.

```
let virtualPrivateSpace = taxAgency.platform
```

The lawyer/accountant can recommend a notary nearby. If I prefer to choose the notary myself, the complete list of notaries is available on the website of the National Union of Public Notaries in Romania.

```
var notary: Bool = true
```

Here is a Power of Attorney template that I can freely use for any accounting firm and notary:

```
var mandate: String = ""
```

POWER OF ATTORNEY

I, the undersigned, ..., citizen ...., domiciled in ...., holder of passport / ID series ...., nr ...., issued by ...., at ...., valid until ...., in my quality of legal representative of the company ...., tax ID ...., Trade Registry number ...., address ....,

hereby authorise ...., Romanian citizen, domiciled in ...., CNP ...., ID series .... no. .... / .... issued by ....,

RULE 4. I GET A GOOD ACCOUNTANT

in the name and on behalf of the mandating company, to prepare and submit the tax returns of the company, listed in the Order of The Romanian National Agency of Tax Administration (ANAF) no. 2520/2010, by electronic means, using the "On-line statement" service available on the website of the Ministry of Public Finance, the portal of ANAF.

Also, the trustee is empowered to sign and file the request for the use of a digital certificate (Form 150), in the name and on behalf of the company, to access the tax profile of the company in accordance with the provisions of the ANAF Order no. 230/07.03.2013 approving the procedure for accessing the information contained in the taxpayer's tax profile.

At the same time, I mandate my trustee to have access to the tax profile of SPV (virtual private space) according to art.15 par. 9 lit. a), b), c) of Order no. 660 / 2017 of the Ministry of Public Finance.

To fulfil this mandate, the trustee will sign validly on behalf of the company in front of any natural or legal person, will be able to make any kind of requests or statements, will file and collect any kind of documents, including tax returns in electronic format, will sign and file all documents and statements filed in electronic format, will pay any taxes, its signature being binding on the company.

Written and edited today, the date of authentication of this document, in a single original, which was retained in the notary office archive.

SIGNATURE,

Do I need to have an interpreter?

When I go to the notary, if I do not understand Romanian, I will need to have a certified translator with me, in the role of interpreter. Most notaries work with one or more translators, so I can make a reservation in advance for both the notary and the interpreter. If I want to choose the interpreter myself, the list of certified translators is available on the website of the Ministry of Justice.

```
var interpreter: Bool?
```

The first steps in the accounting of my business in Romania

From the first moment after I start my business in Romania, some important deadlines start to run, after which my company is exposed to fines and penalties. The accountant or accounting firm I have chosen will take a few steps for me: offering me the KYC form, according to the procedures of the National Office for Prevention and Combating Money Laundering; registering my company with the Tax Agency; and purchasing the Inspection Register for my business in Romania, if my lawyer has not already purchased it.

```
var inspectionRegister =
inspectionRegister.myBusinessInRomania
```

The accountant will also take care of obtaining the VAT code for my business in Romania.

RULE 4. I GET A GOOD ACCOUNTANT

How do I get the VAT code?

Obtaining the VAT code has several advantages: it will allow me to do business with other companies in the European Union - and I will be able to claim VAT on reimbursement for invoices I receive from my business partners in Romania who are registered for VAT.

```
var vatCode: Bool?
```

Below I will read about 5 cases of obtaining the VAT code: 1) at the launch of the business - or at any time up to the threshold of RON 300 000; 2) above the threshold of RON 300 000; 3) the special VAT code for intra-Community transactions; 4) VAT code for e-commerce; 5) the recovery of a lost VAT code.

1. The VAT code at the launch of the business - or at any time up to the threshold of RON 300 000

Obtaining the VAT code once the business is launched - or at any time up to the threshold of RON 300 000 - is called *"registration for VAT purposes by expressing an option"*.

```
var optionalVatCode: Bool?
```

The list of documents I have to submit to get this optional VAT code includes a Statement on my own responsibility for the VAT registration. It is the best to fill it in together with my accountant or tax consultant, to sign it, then my accountant or tax consultant uploads it on the Tax Agency platform. Also, my accountant will fill a Statement of mentions – Tax Form 010 on my behalf, which can be filled in by my accountant.

MY BUSINESS IN ROMANIA™

I also need to attach a proof of submission of the Statement on my own responsibility without validation errors.

Typical reasons for rejecting my application for a VAT code include being in insolvency, or if the contract for the company's registered office is with a law firm. If the contract for the company's registered office has a short duration, less than one year, then the application is also rejected. In case I have a criminal record, for deeds sanctioned by the fiscal, accounting or customs legislation - and by the one regarding the financial discipline - then the application is rejected as well.

```
var solvency: Bool?
```

2. The VAT code above the threshold of RON 300 000

I have to register my business for VAT purposes in 10 days after it exceeds the revenue threshold of RON 300 000.

```
var standardVatCode: Bool?
```

If I do not have a Romanian Personal Numeric Code (=ro. Cod Numeric Personal, CNP), obtaining the VAT code for my business in Romania is done in two stages:

A. I must register with the Tax Agency as a natural person, obtaining a foreigner's tax identification number (NIF). The documents I need to present to the tax authorities include the Tax Form 030 for the tax registration of the individuals who do not have a Romanian Personal Numerical Code; a copy of my ID; a copy of the Certificat de Înregistrare (CUI) (=en. Registration Certificate) from the Trade Registry; a copy of the Certificat Constatator forma extinsă (=en. extended format of the Trade

RULE 4. I GET A GOOD ACCOUNTANT

Registry Statement); Power of Attorney & a copy of the ID of the delegate if I mandate someone to get the code on my behalf.

B. I submit the file for obtaining the VAT code for my business in Romania. The documents I have to present to the tax authorities include the Tax Form 010; a trial balance showing the passing of the threshold; my ID; the IDs of the other shareholders, if any; a copy of the Certificat de Înregistrare (CUI) (=en. Registration Certificate) from the Trade Registry; a copy of the Certificat Constatator forma extinsă (=en. extended format of the Trade Registry Statement); a copy of the Act Constitutiv (=en. Articles of Association); a bank statement for my business in Romania (proof of having a business current account, not just the social capital account); a copy of the rent contract, with a duration of more than 1 year; a written statement on my own responsibility for VAT registration; a written statement on my own responsibility that I am not an associate/administrator for another company in Romania which is in insolvency/bankruptcy; a written statement on my own responsibility that I do not have a criminal record; a written statement on my own responsibility that I have not been a shareholder in another Romanian company which got its VAT code cancelled; Power of Attorney and a copy of the ID of the trustee.

3. Special VAT code for intra-Community transactions

My business in Romania is not registered as a VAT payer, but I have to make a one-off transaction with a company from the EU, outside of Romania.

Normally I should register my business in Romania for VAT purposes - but there is also an alternative: the special VAT code for intra-community transactions.

```
var specialEuVatCode: Bool?
```

After obtaining this special VAT code I will pay 19% VAT in Romania for the intra-community transaction when I buy something from an EU supplier, but I will not be registered as a standard VAT payer for transactions with other companies from Romania. Getting this VAT code involves a visit to the Tax Agency with a set of documents (Tax Form 091, Power of Attorney, recent trial balance - plus a Power of Attorney and the ID of my delegate, if I am sending somebody else on my behalf), and it takes 1 week to obtain. When it is ready, I will need to go there again to pick it up, either myself or my delegate.

4. VAT code for e-commerce

This type of VAT code is for companies outside Romania that sell in Romania, by means of distance selling, above the threshold of EUR 25 000 (the equivalent of RON 118 000).

```
var eCommerceVatCode: Bool?
```

The documents I have to present to the tax authorities include a mandate, in Romanian, for the accounting firm that will represent my business outside Romania (Company A) for the purposes of the VAT registration: Company A empowers Company B to represent Company A in front of theTax Agency for the obtaining of the VAT code, in original; a legalised copy of the VAT code of my Business outside Romania (Company A) from the country of origin of Company A, accompanied by a translation in Romanian by a legalised translator; a Statement on my own responsibility, in Romanian, about the type of activity I want to run in Romania; copies from a couple of invoices, so that the Tax Agency sees that I have invoiced in Romania; a sales ledger for the current year, in original; If applicable: a copy of the courier contract with which I deliver the goods. The Tax Form 015 will be filled in by my accounting firm in Romania and filed in original, together with the rest of the documents above.

RULE 4. I GET A GOOD ACCOUNTANT

5. How do I recover the VAT code if I lost it

Regaining the VAT code takes longer than getting it in the first place, because the tax inspectors are more alert to potential irregularities, even if the initial loss of the VAT code has just been the result of a missed deadline.

Therefore, the best thing to do is to take care of the VAT code once obtained: I must not lose it.

If, however, I manage to lose it, getting it back is not impossible: it just involves some additional steps and documents.

I will have to fill in the Tax Form 099 in 2 copies and to prepare a copy of the Trade Registry Registration Certificate (=*ro.* Certificat de Înregistrare); a Statement on my own responsibility declaring the actual place of running the business; a Statement that I have not performed criminal activities (if it is not already drafted by me in Romanian, this statement needs to be translated and legalised in Romanian); a copy of my ID (if it is not already in Romanian, this also needs to be translated and legalised in Romanian); Power of Attorney for the person who will physically file the VAT re-registration; a copy of the ID of the person who will physically file the VAT re-registration; the original Tax Registration Certificate (=*ro.* Certificat de Înregistrare Fiscală).

....
```
var recoveredVATCode: Bool?
```
....

These are the main ways to obtain - or recover - the VAT code. At the same time, it is good to know what it is for me to have a VAT code. One of the main reasons: the deductibility of expenses.

MY BUSINESS IN ROMANIA™

Deductible expense or not? 5 examples

An expense is deductible only if it is related to the business, is properly documented - and is recorded in the accounting on time.

```
var expense.isDeductible: Bool?
```

The complete set of documents that I have to present monthly to the accountant includes, from case to case, bank statements, invoices, service reception notes (=*ro.* proces-verbal), as well as cash receipts, fuel receipts and additional travel documents. In detail:

1. Bank statements

I have to provide the accountant with the monthly bank statements for each of my company's accounts - and in chronological order.

```
var bankStatement: Bool = true
```

Depending on the level of IT integration with my accountant, I can send the bank statements printed, or by email, or there are cases where the accounting software can be linked to my business bank accounts in real-time, making it much easier for processing. Since the deadline to file tax returns is 25, every month for the previous month, and an accounting firm that offers outsourced services has a higher number of clients, I must make sure that I send the account statements as soon as possible after the end of the month, ideally in the first days, to be properly processed.

2. The invoices I issue

```
var invoice: Bool = true
```

RULE 4. I GET A GOOD ACCOUNTANT

Again, this depends on the level of technological integration between the software which I use for invoicing - and the accounting software used by my accountant. Either I print them - or email them, or, ideally, the two pieces of software are communicating to each other via an API.

If they are not yet integrated, then I must present the actual invoices to my accountant, either in hardcopy or softcopy, in chronological order, including the credit notes (i.e. the cancelled invoices). My accountant declares all invoices in Tax Form 394. As of September 2020, I must also submit a monthly statement on related party transactions.

```
var taxForm394: Bool = true
```

The invoices I issue having as object services need to be accompanied by service reception notes. For unrecorded revenue, i.e. the services I rendered but not yet invoiced, I need to offer my accountant supporting documents, such as service reception notes. The service reception note is a document related to the collecting of the VAT - and it is very important for the companies which are VAT payers.

> For example, I provide IT services and the services were received on 20 August. I issue the invoice on 6 September. VAT is due for August, not September.

3. The bills I receive

```
var bill: Bool = true
```

These must be accompanied by the service reception notes for the reception of services and by the contract.

A special case is represented by *protocol expenses*: I must provide supporting documents to justify these expenses: not only the receipt, which must include my company's tax ID, but also documentation before and after the meeting, justifying its connection to my business.

To be deductible, all protocol expenses must be directly related to the company's core business. All restaurant costs which need to be deducted must be accompanied by an internal note beforehand, and by a report afterwards: participants & scope of the meeting.

4. Cash receipts

```
var receipt: Bool = true
```

The total amount of cash payments cannot exceed the amount of RON 10 000 / day. This ceiling also includes travel expense accounts. It is not possible to pay/receive in cash more than RON 5 000 for an invoice.

> For example, I issue an invoice of RON 10 000, for which I receive RON 5 000 on 31 August and RON 5 000 on 1 September. This is wrong and the fine is between RON 3 000 and RON 4 500. The legal basis is the Law 70/2015 for strengthening the financial discipline regarding cash received and cash payment operations.

5. Supporting documents for travel expenses

If I intend to deduct travel costs with fuel, then I need to have travel documents (=*ro.* foi de parcurs).

```
var transportDocuments: Bool?
```

RULE 4. I GET A GOOD ACCOUNTANT

If I cannot present travel documents, then I am only entitled to deduct half of the VAT. If my firm is a profit-tax payer, then the expense with the fuel itself will only be deductible 50%. The travel documents need to display the following information: category of the vehicle; reason for the trip; destination; the number of kilometres; the company standard fuel consumption per kilometre.

The fuel receipts must include the tax code - with the prefix RO, if my business is VAT-payer - and must include the car licence plate number. The total volume of fuel purchased in a month must correspond to the total volume of fuel listed in the travel documents.

The quantity of fuel used is calculated in the following way: the number of kilometres times the company standard fuel consumption per kilometre must equal the quantity from the fuel receipts handed over to my accountant.

If I have trips abroad in the interest of work and I have the quality of employee, then I have the right to a daily allowance (per diem). The daily allowance for travel to EU countries can be granted up to the level of 2.5 x EUR 35 per day = EUR 87.5 per day. The difference granted above this level will be taxed and will appear in the Salary Statement. Complete list of countries: Government Decision 518/1995, updated.

```
var perDiem: Bool?
```

Invoices to be paid, transport costs... But my company has just started working, the first invoices I issued to my clients have not yet become overdue. And then how do I have money in the company with which I can pay the bills from my suppliers on time?

MY BUSINESS IN ROMANIA™

The first money in the company: to lend my business?

For my business in Romania to work, it will need money. After issuing the first invoices, the money will start coming from customers. But, in the beginning, the most likely source of money for the company will be either me or my associates. And, most likely, it will be in the form of a loan from me, as an associate, to the company.

```
var shareholderLoan: Bool?
```

In order to be able to lend the company there is a procedure that must be applied. This procedure also includes elements relating to anti-money laundering and joint efforts to combat terrorist financing. There are certain thresholds that I need to know about. My accountant can tell me more. The same can be said about the inventory, which will become important at certain key moments - and which I will have to review once a year anyway.

The first piece of inventory

For each inventory item that enters the company, I have to maintain a quantitative-based and a value-based accounting. I have to make Internal Receipt Notes and use Consumption Notes.

```
var inventory: Bool = true
var internalReceptionNote: Bool = true
var consumptionNote: Bool = true
```

My accountant will keep me posted on the pace of inventory - as well as the pace of taxes and duties.

RULE 4. I GET A GOOD ACCOUNTANT

Online tax calendar

No matter how much I trust my new accountant, it is always a good idea to familiarise myself with the official tax calendar and deadlines.

```
let taxCalendar = taxAgency.calendar
```

The Tax Agency platform has a very useful accessibility function - reading the text aloud. The *Listen* button at the top left of the page will do just that. I can read either the entire page - or just the part I select.

```
property taxCalendar.accessibility
```

Beyond the tax calendar, however, there are certain things that the Tax Agency expects me to do on my own initiative, not only because they have reached a deadline. One of them: communicating any change in the basic characteristics of my business in Romania. And not only the Tax Agency has this expectation, but also the Trade Registry.

When moving office

When I move my office, I have to do two things: 1) to notify my lawyer, so that the lawyer can keep in touch with the Trade Registry and ensure that the companies' database is updated; and 2) to notify my accountant so that the accountant can keep in touch with the tax authorities and ensure that the tax database is updated.

```
func change (office: Bool) {
    registeredOffice = new.registeredOffice
}
```

MY BUSINESS IN ROMANIA™

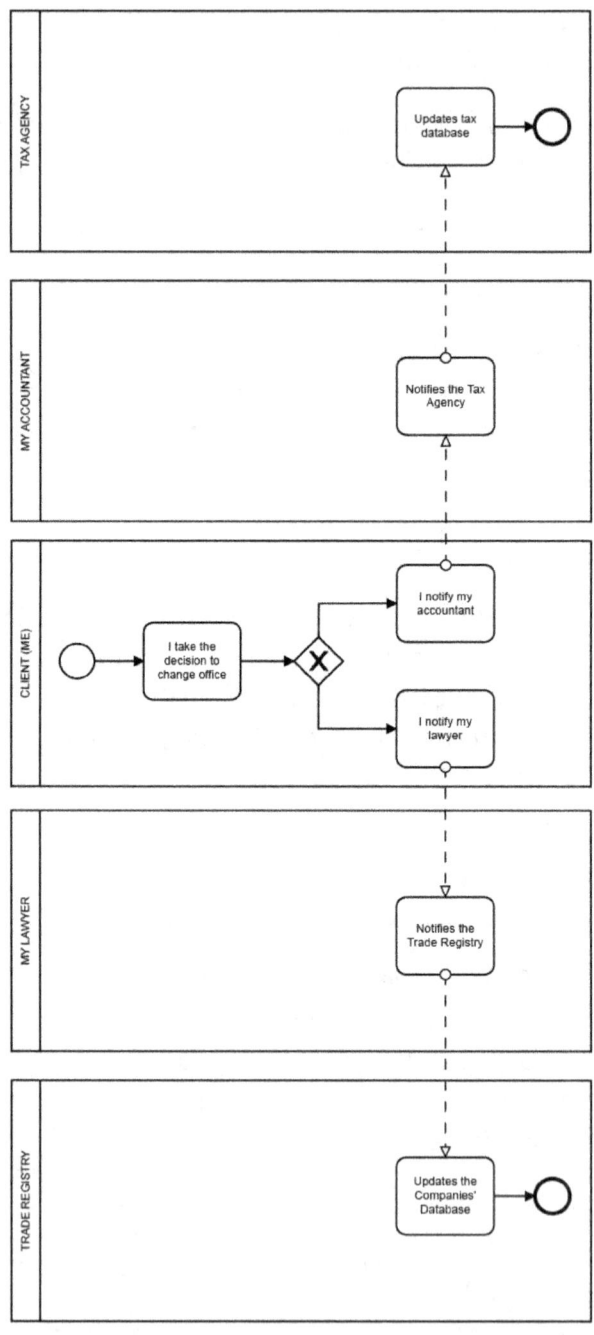

RULE 4. I GET A GOOD ACCOUNTANT

If I do not do both, I may be surprised to receive an official letter that I need to update my data.

◆◆◆

MY BUSINESS IN ROMANIA™

Having already more comfort and a better understanding of accounting, it is time to think about whether I can run the business on my own - or if I need a team. I have to choose carefully so that the decision remains an investment and does not turn into a cost. As I will find out later, there may even be tax advantages for hiring personnel. But, for a start, let's see how I can hire my first employee - or if I have other ways to attract talent.

RULE 5. I PUT TOGETHER A GOOD TEAM

E specially in times of crisis, I need to be aware that even the most devoted people will put their own person and family first, as the owner of New York's - and the world's - most famous 3-star Michelin restaurant had to discover at the beginning of the COVID-19 pandemic.

If I can run my business without employees and make enough profit, it is great. But in most cases, I will need to identify the best talent and develop a team. I need to do it with the understanding that nothing is permanent.

Many of those who would come to work in my team prefer the stability they perceive from having an employment contract of indefinite duration, which would give them more confidence: an employment contract gives them the opportunity to take a loan, to buy a house, to think long term. Using the services of an accounting firm can help a lot: larger accounting firms have recruitment departments to simplify my search - and they can also offer payroll services after I hire my first employee.

The minimum gross salary in Romania is below EUR 500 per month, of which about 45% are taxes, but the employment contract is not the only way to benefit from the services of a Romanian expert: some people prefer the flexibility to offer their services either as a liberal profession, sole trader, PFA, or may even have their own company so as to provide me with Business-to-Business (B2B) services. Thus, they can offer their services to multiple clients, especially if the knowledge or expertise they have is unique. Using the services of a PFA or a company will also reduce the taxes my company pays.

How do I recruit?

I need to analyse the main recruitment platforms and understand the difference between the number of CVs in each database and the dynamism of that platform: a platform with a smaller number of CVs, but with high dynamism, may be preferable to one which has a higher number of CVs but is characterised by a low dynamism. Ideally, of course, is to identify the platform that is the market leader, because it will have the best of both worlds: both a high number of CVs in the database, as well as high dynamism.

RULE 5. I PUT TOGETHER A GOOD TEAM

```
var recruitmentPlatform: Bool?
```

It is also important to know and understand the filtering algorithm used by each of the recruitment platforms on the shortlist. Thus, I avoid the situation in which, for the role of expert that I am looking for, I receive applications also from candidates that are not related to the role itself, simply because the mechanism of that platform allows for it.

Some public information I can consider when selecting the recruitment platform: the reviews that the respective platform has online; the reviews that the company owning the platform has online; the market age of the respective company; the profit of the company; its number of employees; if they have a demo of the app, and how easy it is to use.

If the principle *"how much you pay, that's how much it's worth"* is applicable in this case, then it is preferable to choose a more expensive subscription, through which to benefit from an additional human filter, which will give me the certainty that I will receive more relevance to what I am looking for while eliminating the risk of accidentally deleting certain relevant profiles.

An alternative is to post my recruitment ads on my own social networks. And I have to know that my website is very important while recruiting: this is where the candidates will potentially go first to get acquainted with what I have to offer them. Recruitment firms can help me by creating a landing page on their platform. If, however, I prefer to post the ad myself, on my own social networks, I have to set up my website - and even create a page with that ad, where candidates can see the details. If, on my own page, I choose to integrate a form through which candidates send me their CVs or in which they fill in personal data, I must become even more familiar with the obligations I have, according to the GDPR, to protect that data.

It is smart to have a good recruiter next to me, regardless of the collaboration formula. In addition, when I use the services of a recruitment agency, I can benefit from the added convenience of quickly changing employees through that recruitment company.

If my business is depending on people and I do not have the right people next to me, I cannot grow my business. I am just wasting my time. Valid for any business which is human capital dependent: if I do not have good people next to me, it is better to close the business. Otherwise, I will not grow, but, instead, I will enter a windmill from which I will not get out too easily. The daily hope for the better will end up grinding and, in order to prevent the inevitable, it is better to make the radical decision better sooner than too late.

But, by the time I get to that point, and it is good to never get there, I need to know what it means to hire the first employee.

Hiring the first employee

Case 1: My main business is in Romania

Along with hiring the first employee, I must also obtain a username and password for my company from the Labour Inspectorate. Using the services of an accounting firm can help with the administration of personnel contracts: contract templates etc. - as well as with payroll: monthly documents (timesheets etc.) that must be prepared as supporting documents for tax returns.

```
let labourInspectoratePlatform = labourInspectorate.platform
```

An important thing about the Labour Inspectorate is that the changes in their system come into force on the next working day, and this can leave a

RULE 5. I PUT TOGETHER A GOOD TEAM

business in a delicate position especially when navigating tight deadlines. But the employment contract must be concluded one day before the start of the activity, in order to have time to reach the Employees' Register; otherwise, it can be considered undeclared work, even for a single day, and the fines are very high.

Case 2: My core business is outside Romania

Before I can hire an employee in Romania, I need to register in Romania the business I have abroad from a tax point of view - that is, to obtain a tax registration number. I can do this either directly or through a tax representative. The simplest way is through a tax representative because this takes the bureaucratic part off my shoulders afterwards. The tax representative gives me the advantage of being able to fully process the payroll for me, once the employment contract starts.

I need a tax representative for payroll

The purpose of a tax representative in Romania is to handle the payroll of my employees in Romania when my main business is outside Romania and I do not want to start another business in Romania, but I just need a way to hire the employees. This is also the main difference between a tax representative and a micro-enterprise: with a micro-enterprise, there are fewer limits, whereas the tax representative exists for a single purpose, that of dealing with the payroll of my employees.

```
var taxRepresentative: Bool = true
```

In order to appoint a tax representative in Romania, I need the following documents: a copy of my ID; a copy of the Certificate of Incorporation of my business outside Romania; a Trade Registry Statement from the country of incorporation of my business outside Romania, not older than 30 days, in original; a Mandate Agreement, in original.

Then, the tax representative takes over and registers the setup: after receiving all the documents above from me, has the Certificate of Incorporation and the Trade Registry Statement translated in Romanian & notarised.

Afterwards, the tax representative files all documents with the Tax Agency, together with Tax Form 010. The Tax Agency issues a Romanian unique tax ID with a limited purpose: that of paying taxes in Romania for my employees.

The official referencing will be *"[my business outside Romania], having the Romanian unique tax ID nr. xyz, through [tax representative]"*. If I will later want to do a different type of business in Romania, I will need to get authorised separately for that line of business as well.

The bank account

The tax representative opens a bank account for me in Romania, on which I retain full rights. For practicality, I can empower the tax representative on the account, on a double-signature system: the tax representative fills in the details needed for each payment order, and I just login and approve them one by one or all at once.

Employment contract

The tax representative prepares the draft labour contract. After I reach an agreement with the candidate, the tax representative signs the labour contract on my behalf, according to my instructions. The contract will read *"[my business outside Romania], having the Romanian unique tax ID nr. xyz, through [tax representative], hereby employs Mr / Ms..."*.

```
var labourContract: Int = 1
```

RULE 5. I PUT TOGETHER A GOOD TEAM

Taxes

The tax representative informs me in advance of the taxes I have to pay each month for the employee.

Every month, based on salary calculations, I send a single payment to my Romanian account, in order to be more efficient. The tax representative then redirects the money to the employee and to the state budget, and also files the monthly tax reports to the Tax Agency. When making the transfer I have to take into account the foreign exchange rate differences - and the currency risk itself.

Based on the labour contract, every month the employee is owed by the employer a gross salary - with the employer being myself. The first tax I need to take into account, because I will have to pay it myself, as an employer, is a 2.25% tax for labour insurance (=*ro*. CAM, Contribuția Asiguratorie pentru Muncă) on the gross salary I pay my employee. The employee owes the following taxes: a) 25% Social insurance tax (=*ro*. CAS, Contribuția de Asigurări Sociale); b) 10% Health tax (=*ro*. CASS, Contribuția de Asigurări Sociale de Sănătate); and c) 10% Income tax on the difference between income, on one hand, and CASS + CAS together, on the other hand: Income tax = 10% * (Income - CASS - CAS).

```
var healthTax: Int = x
var pensionTax: Int = y
var incomeTax: Int = z
```

There are several other variables that I can take into account, such as the number of people dependent on the employee, meal vouchers, etc. My tax representative will be able to advise me on the scenarios and the calculation method so that I can reach the optimal solution with my new employee.

Frequency of tax payments

The frequency for declaring and paying salaries is monthly - and I have to deal with payroll until the 25 of each month for the previous month.

```
var taxFrequency: Int = monthly
var taxDeadline: Int = 25
```

Regardless of the case - my main business is in Romania (case 1) or outside Romania (case 2) - HR involves a series of documents that I need to know in detail because I will have a role in generating them.

HR documents

There are two major HR functions: personnel management - and payroll. Personnel management refers to the contractual part and shows up especially in the key moments: at the employment stage, at the termination of the employment contract, or anytime a change of the main assumptions takes place in between. Payroll refers to the repetitive, operational part of calculating salaries and taxes.

On the personal management side, it is very important to establish a job description from the beginning, to detail the services that employees have to do, to make them acknowledge and sign the job description and the data protection agreement. The job description must contain both the tasks and the rights and limitations, so as to prevent further conflict situations.

```
var jobDescription: String = ""
```

Qualification diplomas are also required to prove compatibility with the role.

RULE 5. I PUT TOGETHER A GOOD TEAM

```
var diploma: Bool = true
```

In parallel, a very important document, which is mandatory to exist within the company, is the Internal Regulations. In this document appear both the obligations that I have, as an employer, and the obligations that employees have. A mutual understanding of the expectations listed in the Regulation limits the number of disputes and the need to go to court.

```
var internalRegulations: Bool = true
```

In case of an inspection, I will be invited to present employment contracts and addenda - so it is useful to have them archived well. Each employee must have their own copy - and sign for the receipt. Not communicating the employment contract and addenda to employees is considered undeclared work and the fines are very high.

```
var contractAddendum: Bool?
```

On the payroll side, I have the obligation to pay all salary rights, based on supporting documents. Starting from the timesheet, every month the payroll department draws up the payroll and sends it to me.

```
var payroll: Bool = true
```

I can pay the salary through the bank or in cash. If I pay the salary in cash, I have to make sure that I have the signature of the employees on the payroll. It is not enough just to offer them the salary and meal vouchers. If I get into conflict, the lack of this signature will make it very difficult to conclude in my favour as an employer. Even the court will not be able to make a decision in my favour if the payroll is not signed - because I cannot prove that I have actually paid the salary rights. I can present, of course, the fact that I have actually withdrawn from the bank, in cash, the money for salary rights - and that the amount withdrawn corresponds to the salary statement - but it depends on the court that judges this case. Thus, the main rule is that, every month, I have to make sure that the employees sign the payroll - if I do not pay them through bank transfer - and the list of meal vouchers. Otherwise, complaints, lawsuits etc. may follow.

Communication with employees is essential: from the very beginning, it must be very clear what they have to do. Reporting is a form of communication - and if I have good IT tools, I can get my own reports directly, through automation, without the need for employees to do something first - and then report elsewhere that they did that something. The same goes for the planning part: when I manage to synchronise my calendars and to-do lists with all team members, communication is already high, at the next level, and the efficiency of the team as a whole has to gain. However, for the formal and bureaucratic part of running a business in Romania, certain forms of reports are needed. One of these reports is the attendance register.

```
var attendanceRegister: Bool = true
```

Of course, an access control system with biometric elements can successfully replace the old attendance register, but it could be more difficult to explain it to an inspector accustomed to the classic style of doing things. My role as an administrator, in this context, is to make sure that employees fill in and sign the attendance register every day. Both employees and employers must know very well the obligations they have to each other and to the company. A good manager handles very carefully the time that each of the employees offers to the company, in everybody's interest.

RULE 5. I PUT TOGETHER A GOOD TEAM

It is good to think, from the beginning, about identifying an easy-to-use timesheet management solution: all the allowances that employees have, as well as all the days off, must be documented.

```
var timesheet: Bool = true
var holidays: Bool = true
var medicalLeave: Bool?
var approvalWorkflow: Bool = true
```

Requests for leave of absence are particularly important documents that must be on the personnel file. Otherwise, at the termination of the employment contract, if they do not show up on payroll, problems arise.

For example: when, according to the Labour Code, the employee preferred to be paid instead of taking days off, if I did not make sure that those days off are correctly counted, I will have to also pay the employee the days off in case of a labour dispute, in addition to the money I have already paid initially.

The mandatory monthly documents for payroll are the general salary statement and the individual salary slips. If I prefer the salaries not to be public within the team, then the payroll software can generate salary slips, which I have to offer, individually, to each of the employees, for signature. Once signed, I will attach all the signed slips to the payroll. The payroll is signed by me, as administrator - and by the accountant. By signature, the accountant certifies that the information in the salary statement is correct. All these documents - salary statements, salary slips - are the basis for registration in the accounting - in the bank accounts or in the cash accounts, depending on how I paid the salary rights.

If I have the opportunity to use the services of a freelancer instead of hiring an employee, it will be easier for me. But there are several conditions that must be met.

MY BUSINESS IN ROMANIA™

Using the services of freelancers who have their own company

When the expert I want in my team already has a company in Romania, things are simpler, because it will be a simple B2B, business-to-business service contract.

For me, it is a very good model because I will be able to deduct the expenses as being directly related to the operation of my business in Romania.

The expert who offers me services and already owns a company in Romania can make me a gross offer based on the taxes to be paid - and it is good for me to also know the value of these taxes so that I can negotiate better.

The taxes that the freelancers who own a company are paying

The first question is whether the total annual revenue of the freelancer's company is more than EUR 1 million. I may use a sequence of IF-THEN, to make it easier for me to classify. In this case, I am referring to it as a profit taxpayer.

For such a company, the second question is whether the expert is registered as an employee in that company. If so, the expert's firm has the following taxes to pay: a) 16% profit tax; b) 5% dividend tax; c) is optional: IF dividends > ~EUR 5 000 THEN the individual shareholder(s) in the company of the expert who offers me services each owes an annual social insurance tax of ~EUR 500, capped at this value irrespective of the total value of the dividends withdrawn; and d) for the employee: d.1) a direct tax of 2.25% * gross salary tax for labour insurance CAM; d.2) on behalf of the employee, the employer also retains and pays to the state budget owes the following taxes on the employees' gross salary: d.2.1) 25% Social insurance

RULE 5. I PUT TOGETHER A GOOD TEAM

tax (=*ro*. CAS, Contribuția de Asigurări Sociale); d.2.2.) 10% Health tax (=*ro*. CASS, Contribuția de Asigurări Sociale de Sănătate); and d.2.3) 10% Income tax on the difference between income, on one hand, and CASS + CAS together, on the other hand: Income tax = 10% * (Income - CASS - CAS).

If the expert's profit tax paying company does not have employees, then the taxes it has to pay for the contract with me are as follows: a) 16% profit tax; b) 5% dividend tax on the dividends withdrawn; and c) IF dividends > ~EUR 5 000 THEN the individual shareholder(s) in the company of the expert who offers me services each owes an annual social insurance tax of ~EUR 500, capped at this value irrespective of the total value of the dividends withdrawn.

```
var dividendTax: Int = 5%
```

Coming back to the first question: if its total annual revenue is below EUR 1 million, then it is a type of company called micro-enterprise. In this case, the following question is if it has at least 1 full-time employee. If yes, it has the following taxes to pay: a) 1% revenue tax; b) 5% dividend tax on the dividends withdrawn; c) IF dividends > ~EUR 5 000 THEN the individual shareholder(s) in the company of the expert who offers me services each owes an annual social insurance tax of ~EUR 500, capped at this value irrespective of the total value of the dividends withdrawn; d) for the employee in the company of the expert who offers me services: d.1) a direct tax of 2.25% * gross salary tax for labour insurance CAM; d.2) on behalf of the employee, the employer also retains and pays to the state budget the following taxes on the employees' gross salary: d.2.1) 25% Social insurance tax (=*ro*. CAS, Contribuția de Asigurări Sociale); d.2.2) 10% Health tax (=*ro*. CASS, Contribuția de Asigurări Sociale de Sănătate); and d.2.3) 10% Income tax on the difference between income, on one hand, and CASS + CAS together, on the other hand: Income tax = 10% * (Income - CASS - CAS).

If the expert's micro-enterprise does not have employees, then the taxes for the contract with me are as follows: a) 3% revenue tax; b) 5% dividend tax on the dividends withdrawn; and c) IF dividends > ~EUR 5 000 THEN the individual shareholder(s) in the company of the expert who offers me services each owes an annual social insurance tax of ~EUR 500, capped at this value irrespective of the total value of the dividends withdrawn.

The freelancer can have a company - the case above - or can be registered as a PFA - the case below.

Using the services of a freelancer who has a PFA

A PFA (=*ro*. Persoană Fizică Autorizată) is a type of sole trader with 100% liability, as opposed to having a company, when the liability is 100% with the company. For me, it is a good model, because I will be able to deduct the expense as directly related to the functioning of my business in Romania. But it is mandatory that this PFA does not only have me as a client, otherwise it can be interpreted as an employment contract and charged accordingly.

```
var soleTrader: Bool = true
```

The expert that offers me services and is registered as a PFA might make me the price proposal based on the taxes to be paid - and it is good for me to know the value of these taxes as well, in order to better negotiate.

The taxes paid by the PFA

The freelancer registered as a PFA pays 10% income tax on the difference between income and expenses.

RULE 5. I PUT TOGETHER A GOOD TEAM

If the annual income from the PFA is greater than ~EUR 5 000 (=RON 26 760, the equivalent of 12 minimum gross salaries per economy), then the PFA also needs to pay the following taxes: CAS and CASS.

The Social Insurance Tax (=*ro.* CAS, Contribuția de Asigurări Sociale) or the pension contribution, as it is called, is 25%. It has a variable value depending on the income chosen by the payer, but not lower than the level of the minimum gross salary per country (RON 2 230). Thus, the payment amount for CAS is at least RON 557.5 per month or RON 6 690 per year.

The Health Tax (=*ro.* CASS, Contribuția de Asigurări Sociale de Sănătate) is 10% and is due only after exceeding the above ceiling. For cases where the contribution is made voluntarily, the amount due will be represented by the value of the minimum gross salary, i.e. RON 223 per month or RON 2 676 per year.

Frequency of tax payments for the PFA

The frequency of tax payments for the freelancer registered as a PFA is yearly. For income obtained in Year 1, the freelancer needs to pay the taxes until 15 December of Year 1 (anticipated payment) or until 15 March of Year 2 - alternatively, at the date set by the Government, if different - at the latest. The freelancer needs to file the Consolidated Tax Statement (=*ro.* Declarația Unică) in 30 days after signing the contract with a company from abroad, ticking the box *Anticipated income from abroad*.

```
var consolidatedTaxStatement: Bool = true
```

MY BUSINESS IN ROMANIA™

I wonder if I am able to receive tax benefits from having employees. Are there any other ways in which I could reduce the volume of taxes? Let's see.

RULE 6. I OPTIMISE MY TAXES

Whether I have employees, own real estate, have an IT company or even own several companies in Romania, I have a whole range of tax optimisation solutions at my disposal. Before applying them, however, I need to make sure I fully understand what is written in my trial balance and in my annual financial statements. Several examples in the following pages.

How to read a Romanian trial balance: examples

The trial balance - or, for short, the *balance* - represents the mirror of my company's activity. All the operations that I run reach the accounting document called the trial balance. Sooner or later I will need to understand it in detail so that I can better coordinate my business - therefore I can already start by forming an overall impression on the types of information that the balance may offer.

```
var trialBalance: Bool = true
```

At the same time, the balance is the mirror of my accountant's activity. This is exactly why I have to check it all the time. The most visible example is if I decide to close the company - when the lack of assets and the existence of very large debts allow late conclusions to be drawn: either not including all expenses in accounting, or leaving suppliers' advances, or simply subsidising personal activities on the company's back and with the money of the suppliers - all these negative habits will have repercussions in the end. It is good to understand this before I get to want to do exit and actually discover that I have very high taxes to pay, that I get cross-checks, that I have a tax record, that I cannot open another company.

An extremely important first rule: I must ask my accountant to share with me, on a monthly basis, the balance in both synthetic format as well as, especially, in analytical format. It is important for me to be able to differentiate between the synthetic balance and the analytical balance: the synthetic balance is the folded, compressed version, at the level of totals, while the analytical balance, unfolded, allows me to easily see if my accountant has worked correctly, if the accountant has processed all the documents I have provided - and has respected all accounting rules and regulations.

RULE 6. I OPTIMISE MY TAXES

....
```
var syntheticBalance: Bool = true
var analyticalBalance: Bool = true
```
....

I start by familiarising myself with the main categories of accounts. In the Romanian accounting, there are seven main categories - or Classes.

Class I represents the added value of the company, what it had accumulated since its inception. The name of this Class is Equity.

Class II is for fixed assets, meaning tangible and intangible assets which, in a similar manner, the company has accumulated during its existence.

Class III is for inventory. If my business is about trade, here is where I will see what is the value of the goods I have in my store. I can, thus, make sure that there is a correspondence between quantity and value. If my accounting firm also keeps track of the quantitative accounting of inventory, I must also ask for a quantitative-and-value inventory balance.

Class IV is for payables and receivables.

Class V is for cash liquidities.

Class VI is for expenses.

Class VII is for revenue.

Up until Class V, I will find the actual account balances in the balance, in the column of ending balances. Class VI and Class VII do not have ending balances, because they close each month and go into the profit or loss account, coded 121.

Detailing each Class would be useful. Let's got with the first.

MY BUSINESS IN ROMANIA™

Class I. Equity

```
var equity: Int?
```

It is worthwhile asking for a balance with the account names on it, not just their numeric coding. For instance, if I want to see what profit or loss I have, I look at the account 121 - which is named exactly like this: profit or loss account.

```
var profitOrLossAccount: Bool?
```

Two scenarios:

- if I notice a balance on debit, i.e. if a number different than 0 shows up on the debit column, it means my company has a loss;
- if I notice a balance on credit, i.e. if a number different than 0 shows up on the credit column, it means my company has a profit. This is the accounting profit that my firm has made.

```
var debit: Int?
var credit: Int?
```

In Class I it is important to analyse the retained earnings account, coded 117: if I observe a balance on debit, i.e. if a number different than 0 shows up on the debit account, this means that my firm has a loss which it has accumulated over the years, which sits as a heavy burden on my shoulders, and the company, at some point, risks getting stuck and not being able to function anymore.

```
var retainedEarningsAccount: Int?
```

RULE 6. I OPTIMISE MY TAXES

Regarding the debt accounts, I must be extremely careful when looking at the bank loans account, coded 162. If I have taken loans in a foreign currency then I must ensure I have enough liquidity to cover the amount I have in the bank repayment schedule, multiplied with the currency exchange rate at the end of the month.

```
var longTermBankLoansAccount: Int?
```

In the account for other loans and assimilated debts, coded 167, I will find the leases which I took to operationalise my firm's activity: cars, equipment, machinery, installations. Also, I need to look at the bank's repayment schedule, to see the value of the remaining leasing payment: the rest of the tranches to be paid multiplied with the currency exchange rate at the end of the month. In this account, I will also find the guarantees to return to suppliers, for contracts with a duration longer than one year. One of the reasons why it is very important to ask my accountant for a monthly analytical balance, unwrapped, is that, for each leasing contract and for each guarantee to return, I will find an analytical sub-account in the analytical balance, for instance:

- 16701 leasing contract 1;
- 16702 leasing contract 2;
- 16703 leasing contract 3.

```
var otherLoansAndSimilarDebtsAccount: Int?
```

After in Class I of accounts I could see what is the added value of the company, which has accumulated since its establishment, in the next class I will see what are the fixed assets of the company:

Class II. Fixed assets

I have to start by asking the accountant for a register of fixed assets, because I have to see, concretely, what I have in the company. The value on the debit of the balance is where I will find the buildings (account 212), the cars (account 213), the furniture (account 214) - at the purchase value of the goods. If I deduct from the entire Class II the credit balance of the amortisation and depreciation accounts (account 280 amortisation for intangible assets and account 281 depreciation for tangible assets), I will obtain the unamortised value of the fixed assets that I still have to depreciate on costs - and that I must consider when I make the business plan, because, for me, this is a cost that I have to recover. If I sell at a lower price than the one which includes this depreciation component, without getting a margin to cover all expenses, then it will be difficult for me to go further, because, at some point, I will reach a stumbling block.

```
var buildingsAccount: Int?
var plantMachineryAndMotorVehiclesAccount: Int?
var fixturesAndFittingsAccount: Int?
var amortisationOfIntangibleAssetsAccount: Int?
var depreciationOfTangibleAssetsAccount: Int?
```

Class III. Inventories

In the category of inventory accounts, I have the raw materials account (coded 301), the consumables account (coded 302), the materials in the form of small inventory account (coded 303), the goods purchased for resale account (coded 371), the work in progress account and, respectively, services in progress (coded 331 and 332, respectively), the finished goods account (coded 345).

```
var rawMaterialsAccount: Int?
var consumablesAccount: Int?
var materialsInTheFormOfSmallInventoryAccount: Int?
```

RULE 6. I OPTIMISE MY TAXES

```
var goodsPurchasedForResaleAccount: Int?
var workInProgressAccount: Int?
var servicesInProgressAccount: Int?
var finishedGoodsAccount: Int?
```

These accounts always have debit balances. In them are found the inventories of finished products or unfinished production that I have in the company's patrimony, which I have not yet sold, I am going to sell - and from here I am going to obtain the source of financing to go on with the company.

Class IV. Receivables and payables

The most important account is the customers' account, coded 411. Here are the Invoices I have to collect. It is very important to have an analytical balance in order to understand this account: if I do not have the details of the Invoices by age and the 3 years in which I had the right to sue the bad payers are already passed, I can say goodbye to those amounts, and I will reduce the profit with the respective amounts. So, it is crucial to ask the accountant for the analytical balance, to reconcile with what I know is collected - and I must permanently and consistently act to recover the money.

```
var customersAccount: Int?
```

A negative example with very serious consequences: if I have credit balances - i.e. 411 has a balance on the ending credit balance column - this means that I have collected and not issued an Invoice, or the accountant has not entered the Invoice in the accounts. What does this error mean? It means that, for the missing invoice, I did not pay the VAT, if my company is a VAT payer, I did not pay the profit tax or the income tax of the micro-enterprises - which generates costly increases and penalties, which I will also have to support from profit.

If I did not foresee this risk as a margin, in the selling price of goods or services - the risk is that, at some point, I will have to pay increases and penalties, I will not be able to cover them, and they will accumulate in the loss I will record.

For accounts on credit - all accounts of suppliers, coded 401 - I also need to ask the accountant for an analytical balance, in which I will have, in a mirror, what I have to pay: I must ensure there are no bills double recorded, meaning that I benefited from a tax benefit, lowering the VAT, I also benefited from the expense, which, in the same way, attracts some consequences. I have to ask for the analytical balance for the suppliers and to reconcile the suppliers I still have to pay: for any discrepancy, I have to ask the accountant for an account sheet, which we can reconcile together.

```
var suppliersAccount: Int?
```

In the balance, I can also find the account of advance payments to suppliers, coded 409. Again, I have to ask the accountant for an analytical balance and an account statement, which we should reconcile, because this account is what I paid to the suppliers as an advance, and they have not yet delivered the good or service - so I need to ask for a Cancellation Invoice and be able to receive the good or service in the company's patrimony.

```
var advancePaymentsToSuppliersAccount: Int?
```

In the mirror, on the credit side, I find the account of advance payments from customers, coded 419, which is the account of advances received by my company from customers to whom I have not yet delivered the products or services. Likewise, I have to invoice it, because it must always correspond to the maximum duration term of the advance in the contract, because its non-recognition in the Profit or Loss Account, at the maturity of the contract, also generates increases and penalties for non-declaring and

RULE 6. I OPTIMISE MY TAXES

non-paying of profit tax and VAT, which may fall under the scope of the Law for Preventing and Combating Tax Evasion.

```
var advancePaymentsFromCustomersAccount: Int?
```

Salary accounts, social security contributions, social health insurance, occupational insurance contribution, including payroll tax, all have ending credit balances and represent, in fact, the salary obligations I have to pay in the last month. If I ask the accountant for a balance in June, for example, I need to already have my payroll from June. What I have on the payroll as payment obligations must be reflected in the accounting.

To make sure that the taxes are declared correctly and that I do not have any missing tax return, I can ask the accountant, on a monthly basis, for a tax certificate. Thus, I will have the certainty that taxes were calculated correctly, that all tax returns were submitted on time - and I can prevent unpleasant situations that can even lead to blocked accounts.

```
var taxCertificate: Bool?
```

The profit / income tax account, coded 441, always has a credit balance.

```
var incomeTaxAccountOnCredit: Bool = true
```

The VAT payable account, coded 4423, is applicable to companies that are VAT payers - and, in the same way, always has a credit balance, which represents the amount I am obliged to pay.

The VAT receivable account, coded 4424, shows me the moment when the investments I have made in the company have exceeded the value of the VAT collected from the sales.

The notion of Value Added Tax means that, if I do not make investments, I have VAT to pay - therefore, the alternative for me is to bring value to the VAT from suppliers.

```
var vatPayableAccount: Int?
var vatReceivableAccount: Int?
```

I have to be very careful when I find in the balance the suspense account, coded 473, because this is a settlement account where I can find various issues from operations being clarified: unoperated documents, transactions without supporting documents etc. This account must always be zero, not with a very large balance. I must only allow the accountant to keep this account's balance on zero.

....
```
var suspenseAccount: Int?
```
....

I must also pay close attention to the sundry debtors account, coded 461, because of the following negative example: shareholders, who collect dividends but do not want to pay the dividend tax, distribute everything in this account, in the hope that no one will control them. But all the inspection agents that come - Tax Agency, Antifraud - look first at this account, because this is money taken out of the company for which the respective shareholders did not pay tax. The inspectors will calculate taxes, increases and penalties, starting from the first amount that the respective shareholders have collected.

....
```
var sundryDebtorsAccount: Int?
```
....

The sundry creditors' account, coded 462, represents, in fact, the guarantees I have received, with a term of less than one year, and which I must, of course, return to the customers - or amounts received as loans from people who are not shareholders of the company.

RULE 6. I OPTIMISE MY TAXES

```
var sundryCreditorsAccount: Int?
```

Another account that must have a credit balance is the dividend payable account, coded 457. These are the dividends that I did not collect - and for which I paid or will pay the dividend tax.

```
var dividendsPayableAccount: Int?
```

Class V. Liquidities

Class V includes, among other sources of liquidity, all the balances I have in the bank. For each bank account I have opened, I have to find an analytical sub-account in the accounting records. When I look at the analytical balance, I will see that I have an analytical sub-account for each account in each bank. If I notice either that I do not have a value, or that the values do not match, it is because the account statements were not processed by the accountant - so we have to speak to about it. This aspect reopens the discussion with the integration between the various accounting software in Romania and the banking platforms, so that the import of the bank statements takes place automatically, through API, as well as the reconciliation between the issued invoices and the receipts from the bank.

The petty cash in RON account, coded 5311, must always have my attention. The debit balance that I have in this account represents, in fact, the cash that I need to have in the company, at any time. If I do not have it, I have to pay tax on dividends. It is not a good idea to let this account accumulate debits, because I will pay increases and penalties on it for dividends collected but undeclared and untaxed.

```
var pettyCashAccount: Int?
```

Class VI. Expenses

If I look at the balance of this class, I will find an analytical account for each expense. It is good to look very carefully at the account for other third-party services, coded 628, because it also attracts the attention of the control bodies. I must be careful that this account does not become a recycling point for invoices where there is not enough information to properly account them.

```
var otherThirdPartyServicesAccount: Int?
```

Everything that the shareholder buys in personal interest is accounted for in the account for other operating expenses, coded 6588. When an inspection comes, the Tax Agency looks at the amounts in account 6588 and I will have to pay all taxes and salary contributions, both employee and employer.

```
var otherOperatingExpensesAccount: Int?
```

Class VII. Revenue

In the revenue category, there are some accounts I need to keep in mind.

If I have a trading activity: the account for the sales of goods purchased for resale, coded 707, will have the highest value.

If I provide services: the account for revenue from services rendered, coded 704, is the one that will have the highest value.

If I rent: I have to pay attention to the rental income account, coded 706.

RULE 6. I OPTIMISE MY TAXES

If I have a production activity: the account for sales of finished goods, coded 701, will be of particular interest to me.

```
var saleOfGoodsPurchasedForResaleAccount: Int?
var servicesRenderedAccount: Int?
var rentalAndRoyaltyIncomeAccount: Int?
var salesOfFinishedGoodsAccount: Int?
```

Class VII minus Class VI must always return the balance of account 121.

In other words, if the income is higher than the expenses I will make a profit; otherwise, I will make a loss. It is good to think about what I will do next if I have a debit balance of account 121.

A number of questions (Q) and answers (A) appear often in relation to the trial balance:

> Q: I have several companies in Romania. For each one of them I receive, every month, an analytical balance. Does it make sense to ask the accountant for the consolidated version as well, one trial balance for all my firms?

A: From a technical point of view, there is accounting software that has this function, to generate the consolidated trial balance. From a fiscal point of view, however, there are several criteria regarding turnover, number of employees etc. which must first be fulfilled before preparing consolidated financial statements, in order for that consolidation to make sense.

> Q: Do the tax authorities look at the companies belonging to the same shareholder separately or altogether?

A: The tax authorities have an overall approach.

For example, the revenue threshold at which a company must register for VAT purposes is RON 300 000; there are cases of businessmen who open a company, bring it close to the threshold just to benefit from the competitive advantage of being non-VAT payers, then abandon it and start another. This approach is not fair: the company has already displayed continuity on its customer contracts and, suddenly, these contracts are interrupted and moved to the new company. The Tax Agency may also consider the revenues from the new company as belonging, in fact, to the former, to consolidate them, and then to demand the payment of VAT on the entire amount. It is easy for the tax authorities to identify the same shareholder in multiple companies and to take it from there, especially that, recently, it has become possible for the same individual shareholder to be a sole shareholder in several companies.

Q: *What are the most common mistakes that shareholders and company managers make - mistakes that are easily visible in a Balance Sheet?*

A: The first mistake is trying to reduce taxes at any cost. There are so-called business people who collect invoices from any kind of supplier, but not with the purpose of purchasing actual goods and services; thus, these amounts remain in the account of advance payments to suppliers, coded 409, which means that the Profit or Loss Account is not affected. But the resulting high profit does not express reality.

These so-called business people collect their dividends from the alleged profit they *"earned"* by not paying their suppliers, and, at some point, they discover that they can no longer cope: they no longer have the necessary liquidity. Their suppliers place them in insolvency, or the bank does not extend their line of credit, because it sees they have very large, unpaid debts, while having constantly consumed the company's liquidity.

RULE 6. I OPTIMISE MY TAXES

A second mistake is not to record all invoices from suppliers on time, for various reasons: because the shareholder or administrator does not receive invoices on time from suppliers, or because the shareholder or administrator forgets to redirect invoices in time to the accountant. The shareholder or administrator of the company identifies in various files, only after one month, documents related to the previous month. Or, the accountant contacts the administrator: *"a payment appears in my account statement, but I have not received the corresponding invoice from you"*. These invoices will have to be recorded in the accounts, even late, but the responsibility remains with the administrator, and the consequences are quite serious. There is a legal provision, according to the Government Emergency Ordinance no. 114 of 2018, by which the Tax Agency establishes certain categories of tax risks: these risks depend on declaring or non-declaring Invoices in Tax Form 394, as well as on missing the tax deadlines. The Tax Agency, based on this assessment, can classify a company in the category of high tax risk, which leads to tax inspection.

But the most important thing, beyond looking at the problematic accounts as a whole, is to show specificity, to analyse the context depending on the applicable case.

For instance, in case of a company that is a service provider, I look at the account for other third-party services, coded 628, and at the account for other operating expenses, coded 658. If the main conclusion is that subcontracting to other companies represents the lion share, leaving only a small part for self, which can even drive to a loss, then that business is not stable.

Another example: in case of a trading company, I look at the expense account with the goods for resale, coded 607, and at the revenue account from the sale of the goods purchased for resale, coded 707. I calculate the difference and see that it is very small: it is hard to believe that this is a stable business and that it can cover the expenses long-term.

MY BUSINESS IN ROMANIA™

Unless the business is online trading and has no costs with employees, rent etc. - or if it is a large retailer which works on a minimum profit to demonstrate support for sustainable development.

In the case of a restaurant or a confectionery, the cost of goods sold may be almost as high as the revenue. I can compare the raw materials expense account, coded 601, with the sales of finished goods revenue account, coded 701: if the difference is low, then the degree of profitability of the business is also low.

> Q: I have an IT firm and I am beginning to realise the importance of trial balance correlations. I have made my own mini-ERP, so if my accountant could provide me with real-time trial balance data, I might be able to know certain things in real-time, to improve my management decisions, without having to wait for the next month's balance. What data should I ask from the accountant - and in what format - so that it is easy for both of us?

A: It is better to ask the software developers if the accounting software in Romania allows API with an ERP. Most accounting software in Romania, however, does export the analytical balance to Excel. There is software that can export the analytical balance of suppliers and customers on a single balance, while other software can only generate the analytical balance of suppliers and the analytical balance of customers separately.

The visual impact is important: there are companies that have hundreds of pages on a trial balance - and then it is good to ask for both an analytical and a synthetic balance: in the synthetic balance I will see these accounts of suppliers and customers as global amounts - which allow me to then go to the analytical balance to see each customer or supplier in detail.

The analytical balance includes the suppliers balance and the customers balance.

RULE 6. I OPTIMISE MY TAXES

For example, if, in the synthetic balance, I identify RON 1 000 in the suppliers' account, I can go into the analytical balance, to account 401, where I will identify, for instance, the analytical accounts 401.01 Supplier 1, 401.02 Supplier 2 etc. All amounts from the analytical balance, added up, must correspond to the total from the synthetic balance. Some accounting software, however, does not work with such analytics; instead, it uses the supplier's tax code to keep track of them, for example - but the tax code does not show up in the trial balance, one of the reasons being the limitation of the number of characters - so I have to export both an analytical balance, as well as an analytical balance for suppliers and one for customers.

Every month, the accountant has to send me a balance of suppliers and clients, which I have to confirm. It is a simple communication exercise. If invoices from suppliers are correctly recorded, if invoices to customers are correctly recorded, if advances and inventories are checked, then the key points are well covered. Otherwise, I walk on quicksand.

In order to be able to better control my business, I can ask the accountant for a detailed ledger, where I see the details at Invoice level, and I can sort the information on the accounts.

Or, if I am interested in a more general level, not so detailed, I can ask for an analytical balance for the suppliers and one for the customers, with initial values. This way I can compare the initial value with the final values, and, if they are equal, it is clear that either I have supplier balances from previous years that I did not pay, or, in the mirror, customer balances that I did not collect.

I can also ask the accountant for an analytical balance on advances paid to suppliers and an analytical balance on advances received from customers.

These analytical balances allow me to analyse my cashflow, because, always, the customer balance must be higher than the supplier balance; this is how I ensure the stability of my business.

I can also ask the accountant for an analytical balance of expenses and an analytical balance of revenue.

Also, I can ask the accountant to send me, on a monthly basis, the purchases ledger and the sales ledger. This way I can see what I invoiced - the sales ledger - and what I bought - the purchases ledger. The value in the sales ledger must be higher than in the purchases ledger because this is the raison d'être of a Company. The purchases ledger may have a higher value than the sales ledger when I start investing; for example, I had a profit from previous years that I did not collect as dividends - and I started investing to grow the business: investing in people, making applications to automate certain flows, or even to sell on the market in the next period.

Therefore, in order for me to run my business with my own custom tools, these are some of the documents that my accountant can share with me in Excel every month - or upload to a drive. I will be able to automate receiving them and integrating them into my mini-reporting system, which allows data interpretation and correlation with other data that I do not necessarily find in accounting.

> Q: As an IT company owner, do I need to pay attention to certain accounting signals?

A: In the relationship between the IT firm and the accounting firm, sometimes there may be communication problems: everything the IT firm does for a software application (that it registers for copyright, as a trademark, until the app development is completed) must not affect the expenditure, but must be capitalised in the accrued revenue account, coded 471.

RULE 6. I OPTIMISE MY TAXES

Only when the app is completed, only then must it be taken to the account for concessions, patents, licences, trademarks and similar rights and assets, coded 205 - and is amortised, from a tax point of view, in an interval of 3 years. I must pay close attention to this detail: the lack of communication between the IT company director and the accountant may lead to the wrong classification.

There are also cases in which the owner of an IT company says "*I do not want to capitalise because I do not want to pay income tax*" - but, in case of a tax inspection, the tax inspectors will reconsider the expense: they will not consider it tax-deductible if the company is a profit tax payer, because, in fact, it had to be capitalised.

....

Equally important to understanding the Balance Sheet is, in turn, knowing the tax deadlines and the tax calendar previously mentioned: this is essential because it allows me to optimise my cashflow. I also need to keep an eye open for tax deferral opportunities, when interest and charges for delayed tax payment are not calculated - as is the case, for example, during a pandemic.

Becoming familiar with the tax deadlines

In Romania, the standard deadline for filing tax forms and paying tax obligations is 25 each month, with the following specific: when 25 falls on a weekend, or on a non-working day, the forms may be filed on the next working day, but it is best when the payment of taxes is made by the working day before 25. If, for example, 25 falls on a Sunday and 26, on Monday, is a working day, then the forms may be filed by 26, inclusive, but the payment of taxes is ideal to be made by 24, on Friday, if that Friday is a working day. If that Friday is not a working day either, then the deadline is further taken backwards.

MY BUSINESS IN ROMANIA™

High revenue, low profit? I need to try this

As an option for companies with revenue below EUR 1 million, the Tax Code includes a feature that helps: I can convert my company from a micro-enterprise to a profit tax paying company if I have at least 2 employees, I increase the share capital to more than RON 45 000 - and if I submit a request in this regard, according to a procedure detailed in the Tax Procedure Code.

The conditions are cumulative. I will then be able to use the extra deposited share capital to further grow the company. Increasing the share capital even if I have a turnover below EUR 1 million offers me another advantage: a company that starts with a higher volume of cash benefits from a higher level of trust from its partners.

If my business model has a low profit rate but a high turnover - trade, for example -, as I march towards the EUR 1m revenue threshold, I might already discover that the micro-enterprise may not be the best solution, and the option of being a profit taxpayer could bring a better tax position.

To decide easier, I can use the below tax optimisation formula for high-revenue - low-profit companies with a revenue close to - but still below - EUR 1 million.

Without employees: if the profit > EUR 187 500 then I choose the income tax route (micro-enterprise); if the profit < EUR 187 500 then I choose the route of a company paying profit tax.

With employees: if the profit > EUR 62 500 then I choose the income tax route (micro-enterprise); if the profit < EUR 62 500 then I choose the route of a company paying profit tax.

RULE 6. I OPTIMISE MY TAXES

```
var revenue: Int = x
var expenses: Int = y
profit = revenue - expenses
```

Details of the formula

Without employees, or with less than 1 full-time employee: 3% income tax of EUR 1 million means EUR 30 000. If my business is a profit tax payer and I manage to maintain the profit, i.e. the difference between revenue and expenses, at a maximum of EUR 187 500 (i.e. EUR 187 500 * 16% profit tax = EUR 30 000), then I will be better off with a profit tax-paying company than with a micro-enterprise;

With 1 or more full-time employees: 1% income tax of EUR 1 million means EUR 10 000. If my business is a profit tax payer and I manage to maintain the profit, i.e. the difference between revenue and expenses, at a maximum of EUR 62 500 (i.e. EUR 62 500 * 16% profit tax = EUR 10 000), then I will be better off with a profit tax-paying company than with a micro-enterprise.

Here are a few things I need to know about this conversion:

I can only opt for this conversion once - and the option is final; I can no longer return to the status of micro-enterprise afterwards. If the number of employees decreases below 2, I have 60 days to re-employ.

My income tax is calculated based on the income and expenses made starting with the respective trimester already.

Another specific way in which I can obtain tax benefits is by hiring an employee.

Hiring an employee

If my business in Romania is a micro-enterprise (i.e. it has a turnover of less than EUR 1 million) and I have no full-time employee or equivalent, then I will have to pay 3% tax on revenue. If, however, I have at least one full-time employee or equivalent, the 3% income tax becomes 1% tax on revenue. Doing the calculations, it starts to be worth hiring someone at the minimum wage per economy when my revenue reaches ~EUR 100 000. If the turnover of my revenue in Romania is between EUR 100 000 and EUR 1 million, then the expense with the minimum wage for 1 full-time employee or equivalent is covered by the difference in taxes between the 3% and 1% described above, so it is advisable for me to hire an employee when my turnover reaches the threshold of EUR 100 000.

However, it will be not only about my motivation as an employer to obtain tax benefits - but also about the motivation I can offer to employees. I wonder if I may get tax benefits by motivating my team?

Getting tax benefits for vouchers

When I have employees, I can benefit from tax deductions by offering them meal vouchers, gift vouchers, kindergarten vouchers, cultural vouchers or holiday vouchers – therefore increasing their motivation.

Subcontracting

I can hire an employee, but it is more tax advantageous for me when that expert offers me services through a company or a PFA.

RULE 6. I OPTIMISE MY TAXES

Deducting sponsorships

For companies paying profit tax, the latest version of the Tax Code stipulates that, in the calculation of the profit tax, the lower of the following two values regarding sponsorships is tax-deductible:

- 0.75% of revenue (previously 0.5%);
- 20% of the profit tax.

Important: to be deductible, sponsorships must be paid before the last month of the quarter. If the value of the sponsorship is higher than the deductibility threshold, the amount can be recovered from the profit tax due in the next 7 years. Sponsorship is a deductible expense if the beneficiaries are registered with the Tax Agency in a special register, introduced in April 2019.

Real estate owner?

If I own real estate and its market value decreases, also as a result of the crisis, I can revalue it so that I pay less taxes.

Also, if I own real estate - either myself or my business in Romania - and I do not use it for residential purposes, but for economic activity, then, every 3 years, I have to re-evaluate it and submit a report revaluation to the local tax department to avoid taxes up to 15 times higher. The buildings must be revalued through a special report issued by an evaluator member of the National Association of Romanian Authorised Valuers (=ro. Asociaţia Naţională a Evaluatorilor Autorizaţi din România, ANEVAR). If the owner does not register the revaluation report to the local tax department in time, then the local taxes can be up to 15 times higher than the previous ones.

These revaluation reports are no longer recorded in the accounting from 2017, so I need to coordinate closely with both my accountant and my lawyer.

These one-off tax optimisation solutions may be put into perspective together with the broader view of the Balance Sheet, which, in turn, provides me with ample optimisation resources. It is time to look into the Annual Financial Statements.

Understanding my Annual Financial Statements

Having already a good Accountant, I can start thinking about optimising my expenses and taxes. First of all, I should understand what the Annual Financial Statements are, if they are important for my company - and if they are of potential interest for others as well.

My company's Annual Financial Statements are like a business card. They represent the company in front of an investor, a bank, a public authority. They reflect the work of one year - and the results that the company has achieved, both in that year and since the beginning of the activity.

```
var annualFinancialStatements: Bool = true
```

The Annual Financial Statements include several components:

The Balance Sheet

The Balance Sheet represents the assets and liabilities, meaning the goods, cash and debts that I have in the company. The Balance Sheet is based on the final values from the trial balance, where the assets and liabilities are found. When I have a Balance Sheet in front of me, it is interesting for me to look at the following elements: in the category of assets I find goods,

RULE 6. I OPTIMISE MY TAXES

fixed assets, inventories, cash; in the category of liabilities I find, in the mirror, the sources that generate these assets: debts under one year, over one year. I also find equity as a financing source of these assets. The higher the share of equity compared to liabilities, the more stable the company is, allowing me to go further with it, to do business.

What does the Romanian word *"Activ"* actually mean in Romanian accounting? *"Activ"* means assets: fixed assets, i.e. tangible and intangible assets. Intangible assets mean licenses, goodwill, software, patents, buildings, cars, equipment - all goods that have a useful life of more than one year and a value of more than RON 2 500. Inventories are also asset accounts: merchandise, raw materials, materials I need to operate. The receivables - everything I have to collect - are also assets: trade receivables - from customers; VAT receivable; advances from suppliers that are not completed; employees' imputations. The cash from the cashier and from the bank accounts is another example of an asset, as well as the amounts paid in advance for various services I receive in a specific interval - mandatory liability insurance, optional insurance, subscriptions, consulting services for a period of more than one year.

What does *"Pasiv"* mean in Romanian accounting? The *"Pasiv"* represents, in the mirror, the sources of funding for the assets: liabilities and equity. Assets, on one hand, and liabilities plus equity, on the other, are always equal. The *"Pasiv"* includes debts - which can be under one year or over one year. The category under one year includes payment obligations to suppliers; remaining leases for payment under one year (these represent a debt until the end of the leasing contract); bank loans under one year - if I took loans to finance my assets, to pay employees, for the development needs of the company. The category over one year includes payment obligations to suppliers; leasing rates exceeding one year; bank loans over one year - if I took loans for the development needs of the company. Also included in the *"Pasiv"* are the salary obligations - to the employees and to the state budget.

Equity itself is also part of *"Pasiv"*. This represents the added value of the company: the share capital, the reserve funds that I built from profit - meaning that I did not withdraw dividends, but left the profit in the company. When I do not cash out the profit and leave it instead as a reserve in the company, this company will grow, it will be stronger, because it has the cash on which to support its growth - and it does not have to permanently borrow, it is not fuelled by ever-larger debts and by supplier credit, meaning from the unjustified delay in the payment of invoices received from suppliers. The higher the equity value and the lower the debt, the stronger is the company. It will be able to run the business, to hire new employees, to continue developing. The more the company feeds on loans, the longer the treasure hunt will last, turning into a fata morgana. When I see that debts are starting to be overwhelming, it is a good idea to stop borrowing. In the absence of a research and development component, lacking investment and added value, if I am a service provider that becomes more and more stuck in debt, I may not reach through.

Case study: a Romanian company signed a contract on very good terms, with a partner from abroad, for the purchase of products. The Romanian business owner was satisfied with just going only to a number of malls, offering them the products - and waiting for them to pay. In order to cover its financing needs, the company took out loans - thus practically sponsoring the respective shopping centres: instead of those shopping centres themselves taking loans, this company itself took out loans, borrowing and losing on its margin, i.e. the resale value minus the purchase value. The margin got reduced so much that it became less than even the costs: development, acquisition, storage, salaries, management, distribution, presentation, rent, shelf. This eventually led the company to bankruptcy.

Every such lesson I receive must be understood and not repeated.

RULE 6. I OPTIMISE MY TAXES

Retained earnings are, in turn, a useful resource, but only when the company is stable. In case of a loss, it is deducted from equity.

```
var balanceSheet: Bool = true
```

The Profit or Loss Account

The Profit or Loss Account is another important financial statement, in which I find the revenue and expenses presented in detail, classified by categories. The revenue represents everything I invoiced, without VAT or other taxes - the net income I made. In the revenue, I find everything that means services - if my company is a service provider - or the value of the goods I sold, i.e. income from the sale of goods - if my company is active in the field of trade. The discounts I granted are deducted from the revenue. I always find the total net income in the revenue.

The revenue, in the annual financial statements, is composed of operating revenue, financial revenue and investment revenue.

The operating revenue comes from the main activity of the company. The financial revenue comes, for instance, from exchange rate differences, if I have receivables or cash in foreign currency. The difference in value between the invoicing date and the date of receiving the money, if the exchange rate is advantageous to me, will represent a financial revenue. The financial revenue also includes bank interest from deposits, meaning income I obtain from the placement of cash.

When I have cash in the current account of the company, the advice is to make a deposit with it, to benefit from a better interest rate on the deposit account than on the current account.

The expenses, in a mirror, are composed of operating expenses, financial expenses and investment expenses.

Operating expenses include expenses with raw materials, cost of goods, what I used to produce, energy, water. The difference between the revenue from the sale of goods and the expenses for the sale of goods is my gross margin, to which I must always pay attention because from this margin I have to also cover other costs. If all my operating expenses exceed this gross margin, then my company has a loss.

Operating expenses also refer to expenses with services - maintenance, repairs, travel, telephony, insurance - as well as personnel expenses, which include the gross salaries plus the Labour Insurance Contribution, abbreviated CAM (=ro. Contribuția Asiguratorie pentru Muncă) - and the expenses with the collaborators.

Regarding depreciation, this means the inventory value of fixed assets recovered as cost, in the expenses. Taking the example of a car, its value is not classified entirely as an expense, from the beginning: instead, it is divided into equal monthly tranches; for example, if the depreciation period is 4 years, I am looking at 48 monthly instalments. The accumulated value is found in *Expenses with the depreciation of fixed assets*.

Another Balance Sheet element: the adjustments - trade receivables, receivables that I can no longer collect because I was not careful when I made contracts with customers, they went bankrupt, the receivables expired. *For example*, in the Balance Sheet I might have RON 1 000 of receivables, but, in fact, I can really only expect to collect RON 500. Therefore, in the Balance Sheet, I have to reflect only RON 500 as a trade receivable. For this, I have to make an expense - an adjustment of trade receivable. This kind of situation, especially if they are multiple - or if they have a high value - affects my profit: in previous years I projected a certain profit, but when I find that, in fact, I will not be able to actually receive the money, I will have an expense with this amount, thus diminishing my profit.

RULE 6. I OPTIMISE MY TAXES

There are other operating expenses as well, for example with the sale of fixed assets, or the transfer of expired receivables to expenses, or sponsorships.

Operating revenue minus operating expenses results in operating profit if operating revenue is greater than operating expenses, or operating loss if operating expense is greater than operating revenue. The operating profit reflects how profitable my activity was in that year; in other words, what I earned as added value compared to the work and resources I dedicated to the company's activity.

I need to analyse the cost of goods and revenues from the sale of goods, which, for a trading company, are some of the most important indicators. The difference between the revenue and the cost of the goods - i.e. the purchase price from the suppliers - is, in fact, the gross margin, from which the company begins to cover its expenses. If expenses exceed revenue, the company is at a loss.

Financial revenue and expenses are also important components of the income statement. The difference between them leads to financial profit or financial loss. It is very important for companies that have business relations in foreign currency - meaning they use a substantial amount of foreign currency in their activity, they make foreign payments, they make purchases from abroad that they have to pay - to realise that the exchange rate difference plays an important role in their Profit or Loss Account, as well as on the cashflow side. In this case, it is good for me to keep foreign currency in my account - or to foreign buy currency when the currency exchange rate is to my advantage. I can also negotiate more generous payment terms so that I can use the longer time frame to identify the most appropriate time for currency conversion and payment. When I have foreign currency available, I do not have to borrow or buy it at disadvantageous prices.

It can also be useful to have an overdraft line of credit, for which I do not pay interest or commissions if I do not use, but which I can rely on in an emergency.

The Profit or Loss Account is the place where revenue and expenses are reflected, where I can analyse how efficient my activity was and how profitable, what measures I can take to increase profitability next year.

I often hear about tax value and book value. These are two different notions: the book value represents the value that I can operate in accounting. *For example*, I bought a car for which I gave RON 100 000 - and I do not want to deduct it from the accounting, that is, to have a higher profit, but I want to recover it in a year and I simply classify it as an expense of that year; instead of making a profit of RON 200 000, I wanted to recognise the full value of the car, of RON 100 000, as an expense - and I still have a profit of RON 100 000. However, fiscally, the Tax Agency does not allow me to deduct it in full, for the entire amount of RON 100 000; instead, from the tax point of view, I need to depreciate it in a period between 4 and 5 years. That is, I will have a monthly depreciation expense, affecting my Profit or Loss Account.

```
var bookValue: Int = x
var taxValue: Int = y
var marketValue: Int = z
```

The Form *Informative Data*

The Form *Informative Data* is the place where I find the details of the amounts from the Balance Sheet, regarding suppliers, debts, trade receivables.

Recently, the tax authorities have started to make analyses based on these pieces of information, such as, for example, how much shareholder loan do

RULE 6. I OPTIMISE MY TAXES

I have in the company - or what is the cash balance. Based on this information, I may have the surprise to be visited by the tax inspectors and asked about the cash I transferred to the petty cash account. The tax authorities have access to financial information, and they are focusing on companies that have a large balance in the petty cash account, anticipating that the money is not actually there.

If, for example, I finalise the year with a cash balance of RON 700 000, while the revenue was RON 800 000, this is a risk signal for the Tax Agency, which will suspect undeclared revenue or dividends withdrawn for which I did not pay dividend tax. Two cases: the money is, indeed, in the cashier's - or not. If the money is not in the cashier's, the Tax Agency will "*confiscate*" the respective money: it will not actually take it from my account, but will make a report and will pass it to me as an obligation to pay tax in the taxpayer's sheet: profit tax, VAT etc. The Tax Agency will calculate the tax on dividends, with interest, penalties and charges, from the first moment since I cashed money from the firm. Every month, the Tax Agency will issue a tax imposition decision and will block my money that it did not find in the cashier.

The value of *shareholder loans* is also a piece of information carefully analysed by the tax authorities. They verify whether, in the case of a company that has revenue of RON 800 000, for instance, while having RON 2 000 000 in its accounts, the shareholders have declared their income from dividends or other sources in the Consolidated Tax Form; after that, the tax inspectors can request information from the company: loan contracts, proof of the sources of money, all supporting documents. A couple of scenarios: A) when the tax inspectors discover that these loan agreements and supporting documents do not exist, they consider that the difference between the revenue and the money in the account cannot be proved; B) if those loan agreements are with relatives or friends, but the money cannot be proved, the tax inspectors will analyse the Consolidated Tax Form of the respective persons.

MY BUSINESS IN ROMANIA™

If the Tax Agency does not identify these amounts as income for the lenders, it will consider this situation as an indication of money laundering, tax evasion - and will calculate VAT and profit or income tax on the micro-enterprise.

The Assets Register (Tax Form 40)

In this form I can find fixed assets, tangible assets, intangible assets, licenses, software, buildings, land, equipment, furniture - detailed by groups of fixed assets, at the value of acquisition - or at a revalued amount, if I revalued them - and depreciation, similarly, calculated by groups. In the form I will find the value at the beginning of the year (meaning the value with which I finished the previous year) plus entries (meaning what I purchased) minus outflows by sale or scrapping - and what is left at the end of the year. The difference between the inventory value and the calculated depreciation represents the remaining value, a deductible expense, element of the Profit or Loss Account, which I will recover in the next period from the revenue obtained.

There are also a number of addenda to the financial statements, which must be prepared by the administrator and verified by the accountant. For example the Decision of the General Shareholders' Meeting for approving the Financial Statements; the Supplementary Notes to the Financial Statements; the Administrator's Report; the Administrator's statement of compliance with all accounting principles when preparing the Financial Statements.

The Decision of the General Shareholders' Meeting

The decision of the General Shareholders' Meeting (=ro. Hotărârea Adunării Generale a Acționarilor, AGA) approving the Financial Statements is mandatory for the shareholders.

RULE 6. I OPTIMISE MY TAXES

It is important that this meeting literally takes place: in addition to the formal, ceremonial side of this meeting, it also helps in the communication between the associates, both regarding the year ended and the current one.

The generic format of this AGA Decision includes elements such as: the General Meeting of Shareholders was convened on *dd.mm.yyyy*; AGA has approved the Financial Statements and the Administrator's Report; the profit obtained was placed in the category of retained earnings - or distributed as dividends.

When a conflict arises between associates, any document can become evidence in court.

I must take into account the following details when approving the Financial Statements and distributing the profit: if I have made investments in fixed assets that still generate outflows, I do not have to distribute all my profit on dividends. I have to keep a resource in the company with which to cover the remaining part of the investment, otherwise, I will be indebted. I have to be as thoughtful as possible, to keep the profit made in the category of retained earnings. Only when I have made a profit that exceeds the remaining value of the investment which still needs to be covered is it time to start thinking about withdrawing as dividends the difference between the profit obtained and the remaining part of the investment. When I leave the profit in the retained earnings category, I can subsequently distribute the profit on dividends at any time during the year, through an Extraordinary Shareholders' Meeting, then collect the dividends and pay the dividend tax. If I fully distribute the profit on dividends but fail to collect them in full by the end of the year, then I am required to pay the full dividend tax by the end of the following year. I will not be able to return to an already approved AGA Decision, I will not be able to change it.

```
if profitEntirelyDistributedAsDividends = true &&
dividendsCollectedUntilYearEnd = false {
    pay dividendTax
}
```

It is not fair to distribute the profit towards the reserve fund, for development, and, after years - when the company is stable due to the cash available at the right time - to return to the AGA Decision and to modify it with a new AGA Decision by which I change the destination of the profit from the reserve fund into dividends. The Companies Law does not allow this.

The Notes to the Annual Financial Statements

In the Balance Sheet are only the numbers distributed by categories, without too many details.

The Notes to the Annual Financial Statements present information on the company's accounting policies, detailed information on all elements of the Balance Sheet and of the Profit or Loss Account, at the account level.

For example, in the case of fixed assets, I can find comparative information: *"compared to the previous year, the value of fixed assets increased by x RON, due to the purchase of a [computer]/[vehicle]"*.

Anyone interested can consult this information: investors or other people who want to get information about the company.

In the Notes to the Annual Financial Statements, there is also a very important piece of information: the companies that have transactions with related parties have the obligation to enter in the Notes to the Annual Financial Statements information on these transactions.

RULE 6. I OPTIMISE MY TAXES

The Administrator's Report

The Administrator's Report is, in turn, an element of the Financial Statements, through which the administrator justifies activity at the end of the year and details the results obtained - which must be in accordance with the rest of the documents in the Annual Financial Statements, containing the same information.

The Administrator's Report is a document that the auditor needs to see, analysing the extent to which the document complies with company policies and is consistent with the Annual Financial Statements.

The Administrator, in this Report, also presents the company's strategy in the next period, showing if it respects the principle of continuity.

The Administrator's statement of compliance with all accounting principles when preparing the Financial Statements

This is a requirement under the Accounting Law (Law 82/1991, Article 262). In my role of Administrator, I must assume responsibility for the preparation of the Annual Financial Statements and confirm the following:

"a) the accounting policies used in the preparation of the Annual Financial Statements are in accordance with the applicable accounting regulations;

b) the Annual Financial Statements provide a true and fair view of the financial position, financial performance and other information relating to the business;

c) the legal person carries out its activity in conditions of continuity."

In conclusion, the Annual Financial Statements are a company's business card and a useful source of tax optimisation.

There is a perception that the Annual Financial Statements are simple exports from the accounting software, which are then just uploaded to the Tax Agency's platform and that is everything there is to it. This vision loses sight of the opportunities for analysis offered by reading a set of Annual Financial Statements with the understanding of what they actually comprise: a diagnosis of the company, in a standardised form, which allows comparisons between several elements within the company, for example over several years - or comparisons between several companies at the same time. All items included in the Annual Financial Statements of a company realistically present its financial standing. Financial Statements are a photograph of the firm at a certain point in time, useful to present to an investor or future associate. A business card. Just as I would not want to go to an important meeting without a business card, or with a crumpled one, or with mistakes on it - identically I have every interest in the Annual Financial Statements being prepared correctly, with quality, and on time.

The Annual Financial Statements represent the business card of my business in Romania. Once I understand this, my business will be secure, because I understand my business mechanisms and translate them into a series of documents and numbers that express the reality of operations: my activity generates products or services at a specific point in time, while the accounting documents remain for the entire life of my company - and even after -, to express a realistic, independent opinion on how I conducted my business. It is a good idea, therefore, to value the documents I have, the information these documents contain. I will need these documents in various cases: for a new contract, for a loan. They will help me when I least expect it. And one of the cases in which I will need them is the one in which my business in Romania is part of a multinational holding, in which the financial reports are prepared according to the International Financial Reporting Standards (IFRS).

RULE 6. I OPTIMISE MY TAXES

Converting my Annual Financial Statements to IFRS

The Annual Financial Statements are prepared for me in accordance with the Romanian Accounting Standards, but the international group of which my company is a part of would like to convert them to IFRS, so that it can better streamline with the other countries in which the group has a presence and where the Financial Statements are already prepared according to IFRS. How do I proceed?

In order to have comparable statements, the first thing to consider are the Accounting Policies: my business in Romania, if it is part of an international group, must comply with what is decided at the group level, just like each of the members of the group in the other countries. The Group Accounting Policies must be applied by each company in the group, including my business in Romania because IFRS must be tailored at the company level.

IFRS 1 is the standard that regulates the presentation of the Financial Statements, Balance Sheet, Profit or Loss Account etc. - and the way to deal with Balance Sheet adjustments. The IFRS Balance Sheet elements are grouped in a slightly different structure from the Romanian one. In the first year of IFRS compliance, I have to also make sure that the previous 2 years are also reprocessed by my accountant, to become comparable.

According to IFRS, the name of the components of the Annual Financial Statements is slightly different from the Romanian version. Thus, in IFRS we talk about Statement of Profit or Loss and Other Comprehensive Income; Statement of Financial Position; Statement of Changes in Equity; Statement of Cash Flows; Supplementary Notes to the Financial Statements. The Administrator's Report and the Independent Auditor's Report will also be required.

```
var ifrs: Bool?
var accountingPolicies: Bool = true
group.accountingPolicies
self.accountingPolicies
```

◆◆◆

Tax optimisation opportunities are triggered at certain moments in time. There are, however, two factors that I have to pay constant attention to, because the overall value of my company depends on them: cash - and equity. More about them - in the next chapter.

RULE 7. ONE EYE ON CASH AND THE OTHER ON EQUITY

Why is equity so important?

A reduction in equity can eventually lead to the closure of the business. Cascading down, the existence of a systemic phenomenon of negative equity can lead to macroeconomic imbalances, because the economy is made up of the total number of companies.

At the governmental level, there is an understanding that equity must be positive at both company and country level. Thus, starting with 2021, the Government grants fiscal facilities to taxpayers whose equity is positive: 2% reduction of profit tax, specific tax and income tax of micro-enterprises. The additional condition is to have a value at least equal to half of the share capital deposited when setting up the company.

If I register an increase in equity compared to the previous year, together with fulfilling the above conditions, I may receive an additional reduction with the following values: 5% reduction of tax for an adjusted equity annual growth interval up to 5% inclusive; 6% reduction of tax for an adjusted equity annual growth interval over 5% and up to 10% inclusive; 7% reduction of tax for an adjusted equity annual growth interval over 10% and up to 15% inclusive; 8% reduction of tax for an adjusted equity annual growth interval over 15% and up to 20% inclusive; 9% reduction of tax for an adjusted equity annual growth interval over 20% and up to 25% inclusive; or 10% reduction of tax for an adjusted equity annual growth interval over 25%.

What exactly is equity?

It represents the added value of a company, the results of the effort of my work from the beginning of the company to the current date. In order to gain a better understanding of this aspect, an analysis of the equity components is useful to me. I need to see what each of these means so I can make good decisions.

The components of equity are the following:

- Share capital;
- Legal reserve;
- Other reserves;
- Profit or loss.

RULE 7. ONE EYE ON CASH AND THE OTHER ON EQUITY

Share capital

When I create a company, the shareholders bring in initial share capital. If I put a very small share capital in the company, say RON 200, this means that I only invest RON 200 in the company.

If, on the other hand, I set up my company with a solid share capital, if I bring equipment, goods, and all the rest I need to carry out its object of activity - then this means that I give it life from the beginning and the company starts solid: it can already start operating and it does not struggle with loans and cash flow problems.

If I put in cash and start buying, it is even better, because, if my business in Romania is registered as a VAT payer from the beginning, I will save 19% of the value of the share capital. This percentage represents the amount of VAT I can deduct.

Legal reserve

What does the legal reserve mean? This gives me the possibility, according to the Tax Code, to create a reserve within the limit of 20% of share capital, an amount which is then deducted from taxable profit, if my firm is a profit tax payer.

```
var legalReserve: Int = 20%
```

For example, if I have a taxable profit of RON 100 000 and a share capital of RON 10 000, then, when I calculate the profit tax, I do not apply it for 20% of the RON 10 000, which is RON 2 000. Meaning I will apply the 16% profit tax rate to the difference between RON 100 000 and RON 2 000, instead of applying it directly to the RON 100 000 profit. // I do not have the right to collect these RON 2 000 as dividends; they will remain available to the company as a legal reserve - but I can use them at any time for investment.

MY BUSINESS IN ROMANIA™

The company's profit/loss from previous financial years

My company starts to produce, to make a profit. Let's say I made a profit in the first quarter of the year. Instead of leaving it in the company, to continue generating even more profit, I choose to withdraw this money, because, now, the law gives me the opportunity to withdraw interim dividends. So I withdraw all the profit as dividends, transferring them to my personal account. What will happen next? The phenomenon is this: the company will no longer have cash, will not be able to operate - and will start squeaking.

Another example: let's say that a shareholder, month by month, takes out money and leaves it as petty cash - consuming it for personal reasons. What happens to such a company, from which the shareholder withdraws money at discretion? At some point, the company no longer has anything to finance its activity. What is the result? Simply said, bankruptcy. Or trips to banks to receive loans. But the banks, when analysing the credit file, do find, in fact, that the alleged profit was in the petty cash, taken and used in personal interest. The banks will not offer the credit, because the company cannot prove that it respects the principle of business continuity.

Very important: if I collect various amounts from the bank and, from the accounting point of view, leave them in the petty cash account, forgetting to pay the dividend tax, then, in case of a potential tax inspection, one of the first things to be checked will be the cash balance or the sundry debtors account. This is because in the sundry debtors account are recorded the amounts withdrawn by the associates and for which they did not pay the dividend tax. Therefore, it is best for me to pay the dividend tax when I withdraw money from the bank and know that I took it personally and not for payments related to the business. Otherwise, in the case of a tax inspection, I will have to make a choice: either to return the money, borrow it from another place and bring it back into the company, and the company comes to life again - or simply accept failure and tell to myself:

RULE 7. ONE EYE ON CASH AND THE OTHER ON EQUITY

"This is it; I have only been able to get it this far."

This means that I did not create a solid company from the beginning, able to continue to operate.

So, any profit I make and leave in the company, not collecting it as dividends, actually brings life to the business. I can start withdrawing dividends after a year or two, when I have already created the infrastructure, the equipment, I already have everything set up and functional; only then may I start thinking about dividends. I must not take the profit out of the company as soon as I make it, especially not for luxury cars, houses, holidays. That is not a company I create for the future, but only for the short term. When I start my business and immediately withdraw money from the company as dividends, without realising I take the company down. I always have to keep a balance between personal life and the business. I must not mess things up - and I must not think the firm is there to cover my needs from the very beginning.

At the end of each month, it is good for me to consult with my accountant or economic director, to check how much I received in cash and in the bank from clients, how much I spent on suppliers - and what amounts I collected from the company in my personal interest. I also have to ask: what is the status of my company? What equity do I have at the moment? And when I find the good news that I have invested an amount and, this way, I have managed to increase the value of the share capital a few times, that the investment plan works and this capital will start to produce even more, only then is the time to start thinking about withdrawing dividends. But only a part, for a start. It is always good to leave money in the firm so that I can further grow it. Otherwise, I will have to constantly think about how to get my money back into the company so that I can grow it again. When I have a very large balance in the petty cash account, it is good to already consider it as dividends and to pay the dividend tax. Otherwise, if I let things accumulate, in years to come I will put the company in a difficult situation.

Withdraw dividends only if needed

The dividends represent the benefit that each shareholder must receive as a result of the involvement in the business, directly proportional to this input. If, during the year the company made a profit, shareholders have the right, at the end of the year, after approving the financial statements, to withdraw dividends. Two interesting cases: collecting interim dividends - and collecting dividends from retained earnings.

Withdrawing interim dividends

Starting with 1 January 2019, I can collect interim dividends within the year: if I made a profit in one quarter, then, in the next quarter, I can already collect interim dividends.

The condition is that, at the end of the year, if I do not make a profit for the total of the year, to return the dividends that I collected during the year, within 60 days from the end of the year.

For each dividend I collect during the year, I am required to pay 5% tax next month.

An example: the first quarter ends on 31 March; I may submit interim financial statements in April, after which I can collect dividends; if I collect dividends in April, then the deadline for paying dividend tax is 25 May. It is very important that, together with the interim financial statements, I also carry out the inventory of balances and assets as of 31 March: this is one of the mandatory conditions when preparing financial statements, be they annual or interim. By performing the inventory, I certify that the balances are correct, the expenses and revenues are correct, as well as the receivables, the debts, and the assets.

RULE 7. ONE EYE ON CASH AND THE OTHER ON EQUITY

Collecting dividends from retained earnings

If, in the previous years, I made a profit, but, at the end of the year, I was not determined to distribute the profit on dividends, and, instead, I preferred leaving it in the company to grow it - this is the best thing I have done. This is one of the most important decisions: to leave the profit in the company means I want the business to grow, to move forward. It is easy to fall into the downward spiral in which I withdraw dividends in the hope that next year will go better; I do not pay suppliers, I take loans, I get into debt and, at some point, I reach a blocking point with nothing more to do.

After consolidating the business, after creating the entire flow and making sure the company works, only then I can start thinking about withdrawing dividends from previous years: I should not withdraw all the profit; instead, I should leave a part of it untouched. By leaving money in the company, the business consolidates and I will be able to grow it, to continue operating without interruption, and the results I expect from the business arrive much faster.

For the profit that I did not distribute in the previous years, leaving in the company, I have to place the distribution of the profit under the approval of the shareholders - if we are several shareholders; with this approval, I can move on to the next step: dividend distribution - normally by bank transfer. Any banking institution I go to withdraw money from dividends will ask me for the Balance Sheet, for a trial balance at the date of collecting the dividends - and the decision of the shareholders to distribute the profit on dividends.

The dividend tax payment deadline is the 25th day of the month following the collecting of dividends.

Very important: starting with 2018, I have the obligation to submit the Consolidated Tax Statement within 30 days from collecting the dividends. If

MY BUSINESS IN ROMANIA™

the value of the dividends I collect is more than ~EUR 5 000, I owe a health social insurance contribution of ~EUR 500, once a year.

Health social insurance contribution for dividends

When I withdraw dividends worth more than ~EUR 5 000 from my business in Romania, I must take into account that I will have to pay, personally, as an individual, a tax of ~EUR 500: health social insurance contribution for dividends.

The subjects of this tax are the companies' shareholders which are individual persons. They can be either tax residents in Romania - or outside Romania.

When I am a Romanian tax resident and I have a company which has distributed dividends more than ~EUR 5 000 from the profit of the previous year, I normally have to declare the dividends until the end of June - and to pay the dividend tax until December. During the pandemic, the deadlines are extended.

The same goes if I am a tax resident outside Romania - but, in this case, I could be granted an exception if I already have valid social health insurance from an EU country, EEA, Switzerland, or another country with which Romania has signed a bilateral agreement on social insurance, if I present a certificate of tax residence - and if I give a statement on my own responsibility for the exemption from the payment of the social health insurance contribution.

If I have more associates and our company has distributed dividends above the ~EUR 5 000 threshold, then each of us will be liable to declare and pay the health social insurance tax for dividends, separately. We cannot only attribute it to one of us.

RULE 7. ONE EYE ON CASH AND THE OTHER ON EQUITY

During the state of emergency and alert due to COVID-19, it is good to know that I can get discounts if I declare and pay taxes in time. Also, fines and penalties are suspended.

Beyond the micro-management aspects, I must always think in macro terms: the key concept here is *Value*.

How do I increase the value of my business?

When opening the business I want to create, I have to decide from the beginning what I want to do with it: do I want to sell it after a certain number of years, do I want to keep it, to leave it in the family? Based on these things, I will know how to grow my business.

Regardless of the destination, the business must be created from the beginning on sound principles. For example, if I intend to sell it in the future, when I sell I will be audited by another company - and, depending on what they find about how I organised the company and what I recorded in the accounting, I will get a smaller or a better offer.

Any investor who comes to buy my company mainly analyses a certain line of the Annual Financial Statements - namely *equity*. This is the value that the company has added during its existence. The nominal value of a share is the value with which I contribute to the incorporation of the company. The book value of a share represents the additional value I have brought to the company. Also, another element of added-value of the company is the *goodwill*, meaning what I created, the brand on the market, which, on sale, will have to be re-valued with a specialised report.

```
var goodwill: Int?
```

Many investors decide not to buy a company because of the *cashflow* problems it has: for example, a lot of protocol or personal expenses registered in the company books, petty cash balances, unpaid suppliers, inter-company invoicing. These are warning signals for the investors, because any tax inspection that may come, even after 5 years, can find these irregularities - and the one who has to pay is the company, not the former administrator or shareholders. This means that any company, at any time, can be closed by the tax payment imposition decisions it receives.

```
var cashflow: Int?
```

Therefore, if I am an investor who wants to develop the company, to grow it and take it to a certain level, before selling it, it is better not to withdraw dividends. Otherwise, I will only get the nominal value of the shares, plus a small amount. Under these conditions, only someone who has a specific limited need, for example for its VAT code, will buy my firm.

As a conclusion, it is good to always increase my share capital from the profit I make, because in this way I give life to my company, I will offer it value. I must not distribute all my profit on dividends immediately, but leave a part in the company, because that is the amount that I will be able to use as leverage in case of a sale.

◆ ◆ ◆

Therefore, I have to persevere, create, and I will get everything I want. But I must constantly pay attention to the surprises that arise in the competitive environment specific to the market economy - and even more so during a crisis, such as the one generated by COVID-19.

RULE 8. FASTEN SEATBELT

Especially in times of crisis, I need to be aware that things can go at full speed. The laws will be constantly changing and I will always have to pay attention to legal changes and market changes, so as not to get surprised; some of the changes might even benefit me and the other companies in the economic sector I belong to. So, in times of crisis, I can continue to delegate, of course, the analysis of legislative developments, but it is better if I shift my focus towards it and I also do it myself. Among the list of surprises, one may be my first tax inspection.

My first tax inspection

Tax inspections are carried out in accordance with the Tax Procedure Code, which regulates the rights and obligations of inspectors and inspected companies.

```
var taxInspection: Bool?
```

For instance, any tax inspection is based on a Tax Inspection Mandate, in which the object of the inspection is written.

For unannounced inspections or those initiated by the court, the Tax Inspection Mandate is not applicable.

The Tax Inspection Mandate must include the objective (e.g. profit tax, VAT) and the subject matter (as determined by the court). I have the right to postpone the tax inspection for 30 days.

The tax inspectors have the right to enter any business premises.

Any goods present on my business premises must be visible in accounting. Conversely, any goods from my accounting need to be visible on my business premises, or I must be able to provide a reasoned explanation for its absence from the premises.

During the tax inspection, I have the right to be assisted by a tax advisor.

If I use the services of an accounting firm and have the tax returns certified by a tax advisor, my business in Romania is considered less risky - and I am less likely to be subject to a tax inspection in the early years of my business.

RULE 8. FASTEN SEATBELT

Get my tax returns certified

According to the Tax Procedure Code, the selection of taxpayers to be inspected is based on the level of risk.

The risk analysis aims to identify cases of non-compliance in declaring revenue and in paying taxes, therefore triggering a tax inspection. Taxpayers may not object to the selection procedure used by tax inspectors.

However, according to Article 104 of the Tax Procedure Code, before submitting tax returns to the tax authorities, taxpayers can, optionally, have their tax returns certified by a tax advisor - and this represents an assessment criterion in the risk analysis.

The Tax Agency and the Chamber of Tax Advisors have concluded a protocol to implement this article: each month, the tax advisor prepares a certification note (Tax Form 180) uploaded afterwards on the Tax Agency's platform, with an electronic signature.

Thus, I can reduce my risk of a tax inspection by having my tax returns certified, to avoid surprises. It also increases my confidence that the taxes I pay are calculated correctly - and I avoid having to pay interest and penalties.

....
`var certifiedTaxStatements: Bool?`
....

It is good to consider the certification of tax returns both for my business in Romania - as well as for me personally, because, in case I am in the category of High Net Worth Individuals (HNWI), I might be the subject of a tax inspection myself.

MY BUSINESS IN ROMANIA™

High Net Worth Individual? Watch out for this

If I am a tax resident in Romania or I have Romanian citizenship and over USD 1 million in accounts or investments, I can also be the subject of a tax inspection - this time on my own personal assets.

It is important to know who-what-where-how-when:

Who

Which taxpayers are considered to be high risk: all taxpayers who have significantly higher expenses than the income declared in the Consolidated Tax Statement will be subject to an analysis by tax inspectors to see if they have an income they did not declare. A tax inspection can also be initiated.

What

The possible results of a tax inspection for individuals are the following:

- a) continuing the analysis in detail;
- b) issuing a Tax Inspection Report confirming that I am not a taxpayer with fiscal risk (this scenario is likely if I demonstrate a very clear correspondence between the sources of income I have and the expenses I incur), or
- c) taxing undeclared income.

Where

In principle, the tax inspection will take place in my locality of residence. However, at the national level, there are a limited number of tax inspectors to do this cross-check. So there are cases where, even if my domicile is in one locality, I can be invited to another locality by the tax inspectors.

RULE 8. FASTEN SEATBELT

How

During any personal tax inspection, the inspectors will present to me the Tax Inspection Mandate, which contains the rights and obligations of the individual taxpayer, similar to those for companies. The Tax Inspection Mandate specifies the interval of the tax inspection and the documents I have to present.

For practical reasons, the first thing the tax inspectors will do will be to invite me to complete a Wealth Statement, starting with the date from which I became a tax resident in Romania. The statement refers to the assets I owned at the time the tax inspection began - and then how those assets evolved: land, buildings, financial investments, stocks, loans offered, cars, bank deposits, jewellery, paintings, race or competition animals - as well as the shares I have in various companies. All these categories are applicable both to the assets I hold in Romania as well as to those I hold abroad.

When it comes to the companies I am a shareholder of, I have to be very precise with the information I provide. I need to state each of their names and my percentage in each. I also need to provide details on the shareholder loans I have given to these companies.

For example, if the tax inspection is for the period 2016-2018, then, first, I have to declare the assets I had in my possession on 1 January 2016, in Romania and abroad; after that, I must declare the cash inflows and outflows during the inspection period (1 January 2016 - 31 December 2018 in this case), in Romania and abroad: the purchases and sales of assets that I made. I must also declare the assets I currently hold.

The purpose of this exercise is to retroactively demonstrate the correlation between expenses and sources of income, lowering the risk score to an acceptable level.

Otherwise, tax inspectors may reasonably believe that they are dealing with tax evasion: expenses without a credible source of income, or undeclared gifts, or even money laundering. There must always be a visible correlation between what I buy and the income I get. It is best for me to include supporting documents for anything I declare in the Wealth Statement, in order to increase the confidence of the tax inspectors that all my assets are correctly declared. A specific part of the Wealth Statement refers to personal expenses, which I have to declare by category: living expenses, family, children's education etc. After I submit the Wealth Statement, the tax inspectors will draft a minute of the discussion, with recommendations for the next interval.

When

I must submit the Wealth Statement within 30 days from the moment the Tax Inspection Mandate is presented to me. If I need more time to provide supporting documents (contracts, account statements etc.), I can request an extension and be granted one, for an additional 30 days. Tax inspections are natural and it is good to get used to their procedure and the way they are organised. But, in the meantime, I need to have my own procedures and flows perfectly set up, so that absolutely all activities can be carried out safely. And it is not just about operational flows, but also about support flows: everything related to people and documents.

In case of an emergency

When I have employees, I have to make sure that they are safe. There must be fire extinguishers, checked and refilled on time, there must be a visible emergency exit plan displayed. I need to make sure everybody knows what to do in case of an emergency. Also, I need to ensure that the documents related to the outsourced occupational medicine and occupational protection services are in order: signed occupational safety sheets, signed

RULE 8. FASTEN SEATBELT

training sheets, regular exercises to simulate a controlled and timed exit in case of an emergency. Nobody wants an accident at work, and disasters do occur, even if rarely; if one of these happens - and the documents do not exist or have expired - it is a big problem. It is great to always be focused on the profit side of my business - but, at the same time, I need to make sure everything is sustainable.

Shenanigans

When I come from a cultural space in which trust is the norm, I have to be cautious when exploring new surroundings, irrespective of the location. There could be cases when my good intentions could be abused - so I have to keep my eyes open.

For instance, only in 2020, if I would have written 20 instead of 2020 in the name of the year, I could have had the following problem: someone malicious could have abused this and created problems for me, artificially changing the date on one or several of my documents. For example, if, on a document, instead of writing the date as 21.09.2020, I would have written it as 21.09.20, anyone could have added after that two more digits, even with a pen, turning the date written by me into a completely different date, for example 21.09.2021... or 21.09.2019. So, only when it comes to writing 2020 it is better for me to use the format *dd.mm.yyyy* and not *dd.mm.yy*.

This warning sign is valid for 2020 only, because in 2019 this would not have been possible too easily: if, in 2019, I would have written the abbreviated date, for instance 21.09.19, somebody with bad intentions could have, at most, turned the date written by me into 21.09.1999 or earlier, which, after 20 years, would have seemed less plausible. In 2021 this would not be possible too easily either: even if I abbreviated, in 2021, the date, for example, 21.09.21, someone with bad intentions will have to wait another 80 years for a document of mine, dated originally 21.09.21

and modified with bad intentions in 21.09.2100, to be valid. But it is good to be careful. Problems, therefore, are not only when someone fakes my writing, but even when I, out of innocence, convenience or too much speed, leave the door open to the malevolent. And there are other cases too - so I just have to be constantly attentive.

Lessons learned

I must regularly check my correspondence at the address declared to the Tax Agency. If I moved to another location, I can speak either to the post office for a paid mail forwarding service to the new location, or directly to the Tax Agency to update their database.

When I lend money to - or borrow money from - an acquaintance or family member, I need to know that, due to technological advances and integration between relational databases, this information will also be visible to the Tax Agency, exposing the other person to the same type of risk: the tax inspectors will look at the rate between the income and expenses of the other person and can trigger a tax inspection on the other person as well. The National Office for the Prevention and Combating of Money Laundering could also intervene.

◆ ◆ ◆

Some of the innocent mistakes I could make without realising it can bring my business to its knees. By knowing and anticipating the sources of these mistakes, I may have a better chance of overcoming the risks associated with them. Numerous examples of such mistakes and risks - in the next chapter.

RULE 9. ATTENTION TO THE MOST COMMON RISKS AND MISTAKES

U nderestimating the importance of cashflows, forgetting certain essentials, failing to ensure that all accounting documents reflect the reality of operations - all of these can put my business in Romania at risk in a normal business environment, let alone in a turbulent one, such as the one generated by the COVID-19 pandemic. In such an environment, the main rule is to keep the business open, not to close it. And to file the tax returns in time.

Not filing tax returns when the business is new

If my business in Romania is new and it does not have an activity for the first few months, I might be inclined to believe that I do not need to file tax returns. Well, this is not true, actually: even if my business is, say, 4 months old and has not yet recorded any revenue, I might still have the surprise to receive a letter from the Tax Agency that I need to file the trimester tax return for the revenue of micro-enterprises - and I am given a couple of weeks to comply.

This letter will be just a friendly warning - but I need to act on it, fast: not filing tax returns in time, even with a value of 0, is considered a contravention and it is fined, according to the Tax Procedure Code.

Not filing the tax records might also lead to the inactivation of my company. This will be displayed in my tax record and, in the most extreme case, I will not even be permitted to start another company in Romania.

Not purchasing the Inspection Register in 30 days from starting

The first thing that any tax inspector will do when they come on an inspection will be to ask for the Inspection Register of my business in Romania. This register is an A3 register where each inspector adds a line. So they need it to record their work. And not only the tax inspectors, but also the inspectors from the AML/CFT Office. And from the Antifraud. So it is good to have it - and to keep it safe. If I do not have this register within 30 days from the opening of the company, I become exposed to fines and penalties.

RULE 9. ATTENTION TO THE MOST COMMON RISKS AND MISTAKES

Suspending work at the beginning of a crisis

Whenever a crisis comes and the world seems to be over, I have to think about things from the perspective of history: it proves that after any storm comes the sun. Most of the challenges in crisis situations are about money; thus, if I saved money when the perspectives were better, it will be easier for me to lead my business from Romania, even in times of crisis, to sunnier horizons.

But there is one thing that, if I do, it will be very difficult for me to get the business back on track: namely to suspend it, to send people home, to tell suppliers that I no longer need their products or services, to tell customers that I can no longer provide the products or services they need, especially during this period. If I do so, it is not impossible to revive business after the crisis is over - but I will do it with higher costs, and certain business relationships simply will not be able to be revived. So, as a Plan B, I can think about a certain level to reduce engine speed to, but not at all, so that my business vehicle continues to advance.

```
var businessActive: Bool?
```

A business is designed to make a profit from the start. If I suspend it, obviously, this purpose is reduced. On the other hand, if I do not suspend it, but I do not realise the importance of constant cashflow, I risk even more: insolvency. Or even bankruptcy.

Underestimating the importance of cashflow

In other words, I do not handle money carefully enough. During the first few years, a business is still in its infancy.

If I withdraw dividends from the company and do not reinvest the profit, the company will not have all the resources it needs to grow. If I pay my suppliers late, I gain a temporary respite but it will affect the credibility of my business, so this is not a long-term strategy either.

I should not look only at *my* cashflow: for example, when one of my clients in Romania has a liquidity problem and becomes insolvent, the Tax Agency can withdraw money from that company directly, affecting my cashflow as well.

In times of calm, it is best to take care of money. I need to estimate my current business expenses, then to make sure I always have cash for at least six months in advance, which I do not touch, so that I am always ready for anything. In the meantime, the Government should mobilise and help the economy, but maybe not from the first day, week or month. On that first day, week or month, I will have to deal with the situation from what I saved.

One sometimes challenging path, especially in a crisis, is cashflow management versus inventory management.

Too large inventories

Beyond a minimum inventory required to ensure the continuity of my business, I have to think seriously about whether it is really useful to block liquidity in inventories.

I have to balance between cashflow and inventory, so as not to run out of either money or goods.

Having inventories which are too large is far from being as bad as completely forgetting to store what I need, especially in times of crisis. And forgetting is, as I will see later, a very dangerous phenomenon.

RULE 9. ATTENTION TO THE MOST COMMON RISKS AND MISTAKES

Forgetting important things

Various things expire, which can trigger consequences such as having the company suspended - or having to pay higher taxes. Registered office, administrator mandate, revaluation reports, insurance etc. - all these can expire, sometimes with strong negative consequences.

```
var expiryDate: Int (Date)?
```

Seemingly simple things, such as an expired office rent contract, or the expiration of the company's administrator mandate at the Trade Registry, can have detrimental consequences on my business in Romania. Because the Trade Registry and the Tag Agency are interconnected, my business may lose its VAT code, I may wake up with blocked accounts or even with the company suspended. In the absence of the VAT code, I will no longer be able to do business with companies from outside Romania, I will waste time and energy. In addition, when a VAT code is cancelled, cascading problems can occur for all companies of the same administrator/shareholder and obtaining a new VAT code can be very difficult, borderline impossible.

Sometimes, changing the registered office can be a problem in itself, having potentially unexpected consequences: lost correspondence, the need to change car documents, to renew authorisations, to notify the Trade Registry.

Based on statistics, some of the most common ways in which I can fail my business in Romania are detailed in the following pages.

Expired office rent contract

The VAT code is cancelled and the activity is suspended.

MY BUSINESS IN ROMANIA™

Expired administrator's mandate

The company's activity is suspended.

Lost correspondence

The Tax Agency usually notifies me in advance, by letter, when it detects a problem - and gives me time to rectify or invites me to a discussion. If, however, I do not receive these letters because, for example, I have changed my address and have not notified the Tax Agency about it, then I lose the opportunity to find out when there is a potential problem. I risk being put on a bad payer's register without even me knowing it.

Not filing all tax returns

I risk being put in a register of bad payers. Failure to submit tax returns is a contravention. The Tax Agency will also declare the company inactive.

Not revaluing real estate every 3 years

I can end up paying up to 15 times higher local taxes.

Neglecting the 6-months rule

If 6 months pass without any transaction on the account, the bank suspends or closes the account.

RULE 9. ATTENTION TO THE MOST COMMON RISKS AND MISTAKES

Also, if I do not register transactions in the Tax Form 300 VAT Return, and my business in Romania registers zero tax returns either 2 quarters in a row or 6 months in a row, the Tax Agency cancels my VAT code.

Documents not reflecting the reality of the operations

For example, the following case would trigger an alert for the tax inspectors: Company A has a contract X with a public institution; Company B has 0 employees, but indirectly benefits from 20-30% of the value of contract X, through a subsequent contract Y between company A and company B. That subsequent contract Y cannot be justified.

Ending up with a tax record

According to Government Order 39 of 2015:

> *"the tax record is a means of evidence and monitoring compliance with tax, accounting and financial discipline by taxpayers, which keeps track of individuals, legal entities and entities without legal personality who have committed acts sanctioned by tax laws, accounting, customs and financial discipline [...] The tax record is used in order to prevent and combat tax evasion, as well as to streamline the tax authorities' process of administering taxes, fees, contributions and other revenues due by the taxpayers to the general consolidated budget, by ensuring the access to information that reveals the way of respecting the fiscal, accounting, customs legislation and the financial discipline by the taxpayers."*

```
var taxRecord: Bool?
```

MY BUSINESS IN ROMANIA™

When do I need a clean tax record?

The importance of a clean tax record is invaluable. Some of the cases when it is mandatory for me to be able to present a clean tax record include:

- a) when I set up a company or an NGO;
- b) when I receive shares or shares in another company;
- c) when I am appointed as a legal representative, as well as when I am co-opted as a new partner, shareholder or member on the occasion of the share capital increase.

How do I get to have facts recorded in the tax record?

According to the same Government Order 39 of 2015:

> *"the tax record of natural and legal persons and entities without legal personality shall include information on the facts sanctioned in contravention or criminal law by the fiscal, accounting, customs laws, as well as those concerning financial discipline [...]. The criminal record also includes information from the documents drawn up to attract joint liability, patrimonial or fiscal inactivity"*, information which *"is included both in the tax record of the legal person or entity without legal personality declared inactive, and of the legal representatives or designated representatives"*.

The tax record certificate is available online

The online Virtual Private Space (=ro. Spațiul Privat Virtual, SPV) platform of the Tax Agency offers a new function: the Tax Record Certificate.

The SPV is only in Romanian, but obtaining the Tax Record Certificate is very easy even for someone who does not know the language very well:

RULE 9. ATTENTION TO THE MOST COMMON RISKS AND MISTAKES

a) I log in to https://pfinternet.anaf.ro with 2-step authentication;
b) I go to Requests (=ro. Solicitări);
c) I choose Generate documents (=ro. Eliberare documente);
d) I select Tax Record Certificate;
e) I select the tax identification code;
f) I select the reason from the drop-down list;
g) I click on Send request (=ro. Trimite cererea);
h) I go to Messages (=ro. Mesaje);
i) I click on Download document (=ro. Descărcare document).

How can I clean my tax record?

If, unfortunately, I got to have information entered in the tax record, removing it happens in one of the following cases:

a) when the deeds are no longer sanctioned by law;
b) when the amnesty, legal judicial rehabilitation ascertained by a court decision intervened;
c) when the deeds are sanctioned as crimes and I have not committed such acts in a period of 5 years from the date of execution of the sentence;
d) when the deeds are sanctioned according to the criminal law with a fine or warning and I have not committed such deeds in a period of 5 years from the date of registration of the information in the tax record;
e) I paid the contravention fine;
f) the receivables administered by the Tax Agency were extinguished;
g) once declared inactive, my business was reactivated;
h) I no longer hold the quality of legal representative or designated representative of the taxpayer which is in a state of inactivity;
i) when death or de-registration occurs.

> *Once removed from the tax record, I must know that the Tax Agency maintains its history for another 10 years.*

In addition to the aspects strictly related to taxation, there are several other mistakes and risks to which my business in Romania is exposed.

The risks appear either punctual, when, in the documents I prepare with the best intentions, I do not realise that I leave room for speculation or abuse, or general, when I fail to notice certain trends that change the overall direction of things.

Not using the crisis as an opportunity

Willingly or not, in times of crisis the greatest opportunities arise. The moment I pay attention to them, I can benefit from an ascending trend, which may take me away from the epicentre of the crisis. Even when the opportunities are not always apparent, I can use the crisis period to learn something new. This will keep me busy and give me a purpose. This newly learned skill might be very useful to me when things return to normal.

Missing the trend towards digitalisation

After the crisis generated by the coronavirus pandemic, things might not be, for a long time, as before: there will be pressure towards digitisation and technology-facilitated interaction. The very curve of expectations is modulated: if, before the crisis, the expectations towards digitisation had a certain value, now they are expressed more and more vocally, both in the relationship between private companies and public institutions, as well as in the employee-employer relationship.

RULE 9. ATTENTION TO THE MOST COMMON RISKS AND MISTAKES

What was, before the crisis, still a quasi-tolerance for working with paper, is now turning into opportunities in the paperless direction, because the paper itself can be a virus-carrying environment.

It will not be a sudden transition, of course, but a gradual one: initially scanning, optical character recognition, digitising - just as Google started, for example, the ambitious project to digitise all the printed books of mankind. And the discussion extends towards the banking area, where cash transactions were, anyways, a small component of the total volume of transactions; now, the premise is that the volume of cash transactions will be further reduced: physical money, itself, can be a means of transmitting the virus.

The collaboration itself between team members has all the premises to be fundamentally changed: the need for communication remains and is even increased, together with the reduction in the number of face-to-face meetings: people are social beings, so new ways to continue working together appear, even remotely: teleconferencing, videoconferencing, new collaborative tools that allow team members to work together more efficiently, faster, and more safely.

This safety is relative: each of the above changes comes with its own risks, which I need to be aware of, in order to protect my business in Romania. And the only way I can do that is by turning resources into protection.

For instance: reducing the use of paper has as a corollary the risk of infection with a computer virus, leading to the loss of electronic documents. I will need even more frequent and secure backups. Meaning more expensive. The increase in the number of online transactions leads to an increase in attempts at computer fraud. Banking activities were, to a large extent, digitised anyway - but now, all the more so, especially in the context in which the focus is moving in this direction, I will need even more advanced protection programs. That is, again, more expensive.

MY BUSINESS IN ROMANIA™

Increasing the number of video conferencing raises challenges in the area of data security - both business and personal: especially in the online field, nothing is free. I will need secure solutions; that is, again, expensive.

The concept of social distancing can be seen, through a certain prism, as physical distancing doubled by social regrouping in a new territory: this time, socialising and working together takes place in the dimension of virtual profiles, avatars - a world both interesting and full of dangers.

Once in the digital world, team members find themselves on the same level with bot-type programs, other software, sometimes deceptive - trojans - or even malicious - viruses - so it is necessary to ensure a level of digital education for my team members in Romania, to prevent the situation in which they or I or my business in Romania have to suffer from ignorance - or we become the victim of a malicious hacker.

◆◆◆

And sometimes, either when one or more of these risks materialise, or when I inadvertently make one or more of these mistakes - or simply when other opportunities come my way - I may be faced with the tough decision to close my business in Romania. And I need to know how to do it because I will be affected on multiple levels - but, also, I might even gain out of it. Wait: to gain by closing the business? Exactly. Let's see how, in the next chapter.

RULE 10. NEXT IS BEST

E xit can be an opportunity. If I decide *"this is the end, my friend"*, closing my business in Romania should not be the end of the world. On the contrary, it can be a great opportunity for a fresh start. As long as the exit is prepared and performed properly.

Option 1. I sell my business

If I want to sell my business, I may be surprised to find that there is a market - and that I can even make a profit. But it depends on how well I managed my business and how well I value it. This is the moment when understanding the details regarding Balance Sheet, trial balance, tax optimisation and equity really pays off. Fixed assets have value: the land is sellable at market value, and the cars at replacement cost value. The fact that I did not withdraw all the dividends, but left a part of the profit in the company, represents an important lever in the sale negotiations: I brought added value in the company. The company's brand also has value. The amounts from sick leave that I have not yet received also have value: when, finally, the company will collect them, they will represent a cash inflow.

It is good to turn to valuation specialists: my accounting firm is the best starting point. It is also absolutely necessary to benefit from the services of a lawyer or a law firm to guide me on the procedural steps in the Trade Registry.

But I may also find out that I do not necessarily have to sell the whole business: I can consider selling only one part - and maintaining another part.

Option 2. I divide the business

When and how do I split my company? The starting point is the Tax Code - and there is also European legislation in this regard (*acquis communautaire*). The division is a separate chapter in taxation.

```
var businessDivision: Bool?
```

RULE 10. NEXT IS BEST

The Tax Agency is always careful for the division not to be, in fact, a simple transfer of assets. To ensure that the division is economically justified, the tax authorities' expectations are that whoever takes over the activity forming the subject of the division will continue to carry it out: in other words, I divide my company, detach an activity that I offer to someone else - and that person must carry on that activity.

The Tax Agency's attention to this type of divisions is also due to VAT: the division is not an operation in the VAT sphere and suspicions can arise if the company that takes over is a VAT payer but cannot economically and legally justify the division beyond the simple transfer of assets.

The detached activity must be independent: I must transfer not only the assets but also the related human resource which puts those assets into value; otherwise, the lack of reply to the natural question as to who will set those assets in motion may lead to the idea of a dependent activity, incompatible with the concept of division. Simply placing a revaluation difference under liabilities is not a solution. I have to transfer suppliers' contracts, I have to transfer customers' contracts, I have to transfer staff contracts - therefore the whole business, the entire flow.

The transfer of assets is made on the basis of a division project, in which all assets must be detailed down to the lowest level. Based on this project, registration at the Local Taxes Authority takes place - and a notarial deed is no longer required.

```
var businessDivisionProject: String = ""
```

An example: my company has two business lines. I only transfer one line of business. I have to justify that transfer, in the division report, meaning I need to have good reasons. It cannot simply be the expression of a shareholder's decision.

I have to show that, through division, the detached activity will get additional revenue or cost savings, through better management, better development opportunities. Cases: 1) the activity that emerges is attached to another company, with whose flows it integrates naturally, bringing added value; 2) the activity that emerges turns itself into a new company. I have to justify that the current way of organisation is not optimal and that I need to reorganise the activity.

```
var businessDivisionReport: String = ""
```

If, however, I just see that my business in Romania does not work anymore, then I can think, of course, to close the company altogether and start over elsewhere or something else.

Option 3. I close my business

The steps I need to take before closing my business in Romania include gradually reducing the business relationships I had when the company was up and running: talking to employees about the situation and finding solutions for each of them, ending rent and utility contracts, scrapping or selling assets, managing the company archive. The deadline for maintaining payroll documentation is 50 years, and the deadline for maintaining accounting records and other financial documents is 10 years, starting from the end of the financial year during which they were drafted. I can keep the company archive in my location or make use of the services of specialised archival firms.

Closing the business starts with me appointing a lawyer and an accounting firm for this specific purpose. Ideally, they know each other and have experience working together, to facilitate communication throughout the process. For the accounting firm, I will need a notarised power of attorney if I have never worked with them before. Both the lawyer and the

RULE 10. NEXT IS BEST

accounting firm will analyse the company status, each from their specific point of view: the lawyer from the legal point of view and the accounting firm from the tax point of view. Afterwards, their paths will go in parallel, but they need to maintain a close synchronisation, just in case something needs to be adjusted along the way.

```
var businessClosure: Bool?
```

From a legal point of view, the closure is handled in two stages: dissolution and de-registration. First, the lawyer drafts the shareholder decision - or shareholders, if I have associates in the company. If I do not speak Romanian I need to ask the lawyer to prepare the document for me also in a language I understand. This will be important, to avoid future problems. The lawyer submits it to the Trade Registry and keeps an eye on the status, just in case a third party would appeal the Trade Registry dissolution decision.

In parallel, on the accounting side, things move fast: the accounting firm asks for a Tax Certificate from the Tax Agency and starts drafting a Balance Sheet at the beginning of the liquidation. In coordination with me, the accounting firm drafts an inventory and ensures that all accounting balances remain on 0: this is an important accounting rule, that all of the accounts need to remain on 0 before the actual start of the liquidation process. If I still have receivables, I need to speak to my clients and recover the money; if I still have payables I need to pay my suppliers. The next in line are taxes: regarding taxes due I need to pay all taxes before closing the firm.

Important aspects which may show up during the liquidation process can be treated mainly as exceptions, but it is good to know them: if I have filed a recent VAT refund request, the process needs to be cancelled and reorganised. The accounting firm will detect this situation before starting the liquidation procedure, via a routine VAT status check.

If I have an outstanding shareholder loan, I can use that for tax optimisation. If my firm has amounts to recover from the medical leaves and I am not certain of getting that back until the liquidation date, that receivable can be treated as an asset and sold to a specialised third-party.

An interesting case is the one where I have recently changed my tax year but I still want to close the company: if I have changed it to anything else than the traditional January to December tax year, then I need to keep the company active until a full new year has passed.

Finally, the accounting firm drafts the Balance Sheet at the end of the liquidation and contacts the Tax Agency to ensure database update.

The Tax Agency issues the ending Tax Certificate which the accounting firm receives and forwards over to me.

In the meantime, the lawyer has waited for 30 days from the publication of the shareholders' decision in the Romanian Official Journal, if no opposition against the dissolution has been filed - and has initiated the second legal stage, the de-registration. The lawyer has prepared and submitted the de-registration statements to the Trade Registry and, once receiving the De-registration Decision from the Trade Registry, forwards that to me.

Once I have on my desk both the ending Tax Certificate from the accounting firm and the De-registration Decision from the Trade Registry, I am now in front of the proof that my business in Romania is now closed - and I am ready for new beginnings.

AFTERWORD

In this book, we went together through the lifecycle of a business in Romania. We went through many practical details, offered especially to prepare you to run your company well. Thank you for your time, we hope it was a pleasant and interesting read. We wish you good luck in developing a successful business in Romania!

```
var success: Bool = true
```

With friendship,

The authors

MY BUSINESS IN ROMANIA™

PS: Did you enjoy this book? We are more than happy when you leave a review. Or, do you feel that something is missing? You are welcome to leave a review as well. This book is meant for you - so your feedback is invaluable.

ACRONYMS

®
Registered trademark

AFM
Environment Fund Administration =*ro*. Administrația Fondului pentru Mediu

AGA
General Meeting of Shareholders =*ro*. Adunarea Generală a Acționarilor

AML / CFT
Anti-Money Laundering and Combating the Financing of Terrorism

ANAF
National Agency for Fiscal Administration =*ro*. Agenția Națională de Administrare Fiscală

ANCOM
National Authority for Administration and Regulation in Communications =*ro*. Autoritatea Națională pentru Administrare și Reglementare în Comunicații

ANEVAR
Romanian National Association of Authorised Evaluators =*ro*. Asociaţia Naţională a Evaluatorilor Autorizaţi din România

API
Application Programming Interface

ASPAAS
Authority for Public Supervision of the Statutory Audit Activity =*ro*. Autoritatea pentru Supravegherea Publică a Activității de Audit Statutar

B2B
Business-to-Business

MY BUSINESS IN ROMANIA™

B2C
Business-to-Consumer

BC
Consumption Note =*ro*. Bon de Consum

BNR
The National Bank of Romania =*ro*. Banca Națională a României

CAEN
Classification of Activities in the National Economy =*ro*. Clasificarea Activităților din Economia Națională

CAFR
Romanian Chamber of Financial Auditors =*ro*. Camera Auditorilor Financiari din România

CAM
Labour Insurance Contribution =*ro*. Contribuția Asiguratorie pentru Muncă

CAS
Social Security Contribution =*ro*. Contribuția de Asigurări Sociale

CASS
Social Health Insurance Contribution =*ro*. Contribuția de Asigurări Sociale de Sănătate

CCF
Chamber of Tax Consultants =*ro*. Camera Consultanților Fiscali

CECCAR
Body of Expert Accountants and Certified Accountants in Romania =ro. Corpul Experților Contabili și Contabililor Autorizați din România

CIF
Tax Registration Certificate =*ro*. Certificat de Înregistrare Fiscală

CNP
Personal Identification Number =*ro*. Cod Numeric Personal

ACRONYMS

COVID-19
Coronavirus Disease 2019

CUI
Unique Registration Code =*ro*. Cod Unic de Înregistrare

DMS
Document Management System

EFTA
European Free Trade Association =*ro*. Asociația Europeană a Liberului Schimb, AELS

EU
European Union

EUIPO
European Union Intellectual Property Office =*ro*. Oficiul Uniunii Europene pentru Proprietate Intelectuală

HNWI
High Net Worth Individual

HR
Human Resources

IBAN
International Bank Account Number

ID
Identification document

IFRS
International Financial Reporting Standards

IMM
Small and Medium Enterprises, SME =*ro*. Întreprinderi Mici și Mijlocii

MY BUSINESS IN ROMANIA™

INS
National Institute of Statistics =ro. Institutul Național de Statistică

INTRASTAT
Intra-Community Trade Statistics System

ISD
Foreign Direct Investment, FDI =ro. Investiții Străine Directe

ISO 9001
The Quality Management Standard issued by the International Organisation for Standardisation

ISO 27001
The Information Security Standard issued by the International Organisation for Standardisation

IT
Information Technology

ITM
Territorial Labour Inspectorate =ro. Inspectoratul Teritorial de Muncă

OJ
Official Journal of the European Union

KYC
Know Your Customer

MFP
Ministry of Public Finance =ro. Ministerul Finanțelor Publice

MJ
Ministry of Justice

MO
Official Journal =ro. Monitorul Oficial

ACRONYMS

NACE
Nomenclature of Activities in the European Union

NIF
Fiscal Identification Number =*ro*. Număr de Identificare Fiscală

NIR
Internal Reception Note =*ro*. Notă Internă de Recepție

OCR
Optical Character Recognition

OG
Government Order =*ro*. Ordonanță de Guvern

ONPCSB
National Office for the Prevention and Combating of Money Laundering =*ro*. Oficiul Național de Prevenire și Combatere a Spălării Banilor

ONRC
National Trade Registry Office =*ro*. Oficiul Național al Registrului Comerțului

OSIM
Romanian State Office for Inventions and Trademarks =*ro*. Oficiul de Stat pentru Invenții și Mărci din România

OUG
Government Emergency Order =*ro*. Ordonanță de Urgență a Guvernului

PFA
Sole trader =*ro*. Persoană Fizică Autorizată

RIF
Tax Inspection Report =*ro*. Raport de Inspecție Fiscală

RON
Romanian New Leu

MY BUSINESS IN ROMANIA™

RUC
Inspection Register =*ro*. Registrul Unic de Control

SARS
Severe Acute Respiratory Syndrome

SEE
European Economic Area, EEA =*ro*. Spațiul Economic European

SRL
Limited liability company =ro. Societate cu răspundere limitată

SRL-D
Beginner limited liability company =ro. Societate cu răspundere limitată debutant

SWIFT / BIC
Society for Worldwide Interbank Financial Telecommunication / Bank Identification Code

TIAG®
The International Accounting Group®

TMView
European Trademark and Design Network

UNNPR
The National Union of Public Notaries in Romania

VAT
Value Added Tax, VAT =ro. Taxa pe Valoarea Adăugată

WIPO
World Intellectual Property Organisation

BIBLIOGRAPHY

Books

Moldoveanu, G. (2005), *Organisational analysis and behaviour*, Editura Economică, Bucharest;
Apple Inc. (2020), *The Swift Programming Language*, Swift 5.3 Edition, Apple Book Store.

Articles

Piroi (Niculae), M., Năstase, B. (2014) *"Professional Accounting Networks in a Globalised World"*, Annals of the International Conference Globalisation, Intercultural Dialogue and National Identity (GIDNI), Târgu Mureș, Romania, pp. 798-802.

Reports

Eurostat (2020), Tax revenue statistics;
National Bank of Romania (2020), Foreign Direct Investment in Romania in 2019;
National Bank of Romania (2020), *Annual Report 2019*;
World Bank (2020), *Doing Business 2020*, Washington, DC: World Bank, DOI:10.1596/978-1-4648-1440-2, License: Creative Commons Attribution CC BY 3.0 IGO.

Web pages (most recent visit: 09.10.2020)

https://www.afm.ro/main/venituri/sii-ghid_utilizare_portal_online-2019_10_02.pdf Environment Fund Administration: User guide for the Submission of online forms service;
https://www.afm.ro/taxe_declaratii.php Environment Fund Administration: Forms;
https://www.anaf.ro/ National Agency for Fiscal Administration;
https://www.anaf.ro/anaf/internet/ANAF/informatii_publice/informatii_agenti_economici/Registru_cult The ANAF NGO Register;
https://www.anaf.ro/RegistruTVA/ Register of taxable persons registered for VAT purposes according to article 316 of the Tax Code;
https://www.ancom.ro/ National Authority for Administration and Regulation in Communications;
http://www.anevar.ro National Association of Authorised Evaluators in Romania;
https://www.aspaas.gov.ro/ Authority for Public Supervision of Statutory Audit Activity;
https://www.bnr.ro/DocumentInformation.aspx?idDocument=34472&idInfoClass=3043 National Bank of Romania (2020), Annual Report 2019, published on 07.09.2020;
https://www.bnr.ro/DocumentInformation.aspx?idDocument=35274&idInfoClass=9403 National Bank of Romania (2020), Foreign direct investments in Romania in 2019, a report published on 18.09.2020;
https://www.bnr.ro/Publicatii-periodice-204.aspx National Bank of Romania: periodicals;
https://www.cafr.ro/en/ Romanian Chamber of Financial Auditors;
https://www.ccfiscali.ro/ Chamber of Tax Advisors;
http://www.cdep.ro/pls/proiecte/upl_pck.proiect?idp=18614 Draft Law Pl-x 297/2020 for simplifying the procedure for declaring the beneficial owner of some legal entities;

BIBLIOGRAPHY

http://ceccar.org/ Body of Expert Accountants and Certified Accountants in Romania;
https://www.doingbusiness.org/en/rankings World Bank Doing Business Index;
https://www.ebrd.com/ European Bank for Reconstruction and Development;
https://www.eib.org/ European Investment Bank;
https://www.efta.int/ European Free Trade Association;
https://euipo.europa.eu/ European Union Intellectual Property Office;
https://eur-lex.europa.eu/legal-content/EN/TXT/?uri=CELEX%3A32015R2120 European Roaming Regulation;
https://eur-lex.europa.eu/oj/direct-access.html?locale=en Official Journal of the European Union;
https://europa.eu/european-union/index_en European Union;
https://ec.europa.eu/eurostat/statistics-explained/index.php/Tax_revenue_statistics#General_overview Eurostat, Tax revenue statistics, published on 29.10.2020;
https://www.fitchratings.com/site/home Fitch rating agency;
https://gsuite.google.com/ Google Workspace (formerly G Suite);
https://www.inspectiamuncii.ro/ Territorial Labour Inspectorate;
https://insse.ro/cms/ National Institute of Statistics;
http://www.intrastat.ro/di_cri_en.php INTRASTAT;
https://www.iso.org/iso-9001-quality-management.html ISO 9001 quality standard;
https://www.iso.org/isoiec-27001-information-security.html ISO 27001 Information Security Management Standard;
https://www.mae.ro/en/romanian-missions List of Romanian embassies and consulates;
https://www.mfinante.gov.ro/ Ministry of Public Finance;
https://www.moodys.com/ Moody's rating agency;
https://www.npr.org/2020/04/28/847492651/how-i-built-resilience-live-with-guy-and-jos-andr-s?t=1592491105240 Podcast *"How I Built This"* with Guy Raz | How I Built Resilience: Live with José Andrés;

http://old.just.ro/MeniuStanga/Listapersoanelorautorizate/Traducatori/tabid/129/Default.aspx Ministry of Justice: List of authorised translators;
https://old.upm.ro/gidni/GIDNI-01/Eco/Eco%2001%20A2.pdf Piroi (Niculae), M., Năstase, B. (2014) "Professional Accounting Networks in a Globalised World", Annals of the International Conference Globalisation, Intercultural Dialogue and National Identity (GIDNI), Târgu Mureș, Romania, pp. 798-802;
https://www.onrc.ro/index.php/en/ National Office of the Trade Registry;
https://www.onrc.ro/templates/site/formulare/11-10-181.pdf Application form for checking availability and reserving a company name;
https://www.onrc.ro/templates/site/formulare/11-10-182.pdf Model request for checking availability and reserving an emblem;
https://www.onrc.ro/templates/site/formulare/declaratie%20beneficiar%20real_v4.pdf Beneficial Owner Form template;
http://www.onpcsb.ro/ National Office for Preventing and Combating Money Laundering;
https://openknowledge.worldbank.org/bitstream/handle/10986/32436/9781464814402.pdf World Bank Doing Business Index;
https://osim.ro/ Romanian National Office for Inventions and Trademarks;
https://pfinternet.anaf.ro/ Virtual Private Space;
https://products.office.com/en-au/business/teamwork Microsoft Office Collaborative;
https://www.standardandpoors.com/en_US/web/guest/home Standard & Poor's rating agency;
https://static.anaf.ro/static/10/Anaf/AsistentaContribuabili_r/Calendar/Calendar_obligatii_fiscale_2020.htm Tax Calendar;
https://static.anaf.ro/static/10/Anaf/AsistentaContribuabili_r/Conventii/Conventii.htm Conventions for the avoidance of double taxation and the protocols for their modification concluded by Romania with other states;
https://static.anaf.ro/static/10/Anaf/Declaratii_R/declaratie_unica.html Consolidated Tax Form;
https://static.anaf.ro/static/10/Anaf/formulare/010_A1_OPANAF_3725_2017.pdf Tax Form 010 for fiscal registration /

BIBLIOGRAPHY

statement of mentions / statement of de-registration for legal persons, associations and other entities without legal personality;

https://static.anaf.ro/static/10/Anaf/formulare/015_A2_OPANAF_3725_2017.pdf Tax Form 015 for fiscal registration / statement of mentions / statement of de-registration for non-resident taxpayers who do not have permanent headquarters in Romania;

https://static.anaf.ro/static/10/Anaf/formulare/030_A5_OPANAF_3725_2017.pdf Tax Form 030 for the fiscal registration of natural persons who do not have a Romanian CNP;

https://static.anaf.ro/static/10/Anaf/formulare/Dec_091_OPANAF_1888_2019.pdf Tax Form 091 for registration for VAT purposes / statement of mentions of other persons making intra-community acquisitions or for services, as well as for farmers who make intra-Community deliveries of goods;

https://static.anaf.ro/static/10/Anaf/formulare/180_Nota_certificare.pdf Tax Advisor's Note for the certification of the Financial Statements;

https://static.anaf.ro/static/10/Anaf/formulare/D394_OPANAF_2264_2016.pdf Informative Tax Form 394 regarding the deliveries/services and acquisitions made on the national territory by the persons registered for VAT purposes;

https://static.anaf.ro/static/10/Anaf/formulare/603_OPANAF_3697_2016.pdf Tax Form 603 to assuming responsibility for the exemption from the payment of the social health insurance contribution;

https://www.tagalliances.com/ TAG Alliances: The International Accounting Group (TIAG®), TAGLaw®, TAG Strategic Partners (TAG-SP®);

https://www.tagalliances.com/component/root/newsandresources?layout=businessguides&Itemid=100017 The International Accounting Group | Doing Business Guides;

https://www.tmdn.org/tmview/#/tmview TMView, search engine of the European Trademark and Design Network;

http://www.uniuneanotarilor.ro/ National Union of Public Notaries in Romania;

MY BUSINESS IN ROMANIA™

https://www.wipo.int/ World Intellectual Property Organisation;
https://workspace.google.com/ Google Workspace (formerly G Suite);
https://www.worldbank.org/ World Bank.

LEGISLATION

European legislation

Regulation (EU) 2015/2120 of the European Parliament and of the Council of 25 November 2015 laying down measures concerning open internet access and amending Directive 2002/22/EC on universal service and users' rights relating to electronic communications networks and services and Regulation (EU) No 531/2012 on roaming on public mobile communications networks within the Union (Text with EEA relevance);
Directive (EU) 2018/843 of the European Parliament and of the Council of 30 May 2018 amending Directive (EU) 2015/849 on the prevention of the use of the financial system for the purposes of money laundering or terrorist financing, and amending Directives 2009/138/EC and 2013/36/EU (Text with EEA relevance).

National Laws

Accounting Law 82 of 24 December 1991;
AML/CFT Law 129 of 11 July 2019;
Anti-tax Evasion Law 241 of 15 July 2005;
Civil Code: Law 287 of 17 July 2009;
Civil Procedure Code; Law no. 134 of 1 July 2010;
Companies' Law 31 of 16 November 1990;
Financial Discipline Law 70 of 2 April 2015;
Labour Code: Law 53 of 24 January 2003;
Lawyers' Law 51 of 7 June 1995;
Tax Code: Law 227 of 8 September 2015;
Tax Procedure Code: Law 207 of 20 July 2015;
Trade Registry Law 359 of 8 September 2004.

Emergency Ordinances

Emergency Order 114 of 28 December 2018 on the establishment of measures in the field of public investments and fiscal-budgetary measures, amendment and completion of certain normative acts and extension of deadlines;

Emergency Order 111 of 1 July 2020 on amending and supplementing Law 129/2019 for preventing and combating money laundering and terrorist financing, as well as for amending and supplementing some normative acts, for completing Article 218 of the Government Emergency Ordinance 99/2006 on credit institutions and capital adequacy, for the amendment and completion of Law 207/2015 on the Tax Procedure Code, as well as for completing Article 12 paragraph (5) of Law 237/2015 on the authorisation and supervision of the insurance and reinsurance activity.

Government Orders

Order 39 of 26 August 2015 regarding the tax record.

Government Decisions

Decision 518 of 10 July 1995 regarding some rights and obligations of the Romanian personnel sent abroad for the accomplishment of some temporary missions;

Decision 1272/2005 for the approval of the list of natural and legal persons suspected of committing or financing acts of terrorism;

Decision 1437/2008 on the approval of the List comprising third countries that impose requirements similar to those provided by Law 656/2002 for the prevention and sanctioning of money laundering, as well as for the establishment of measures to prevent and combat the financing of terrorist acts.

LEGISLATION

Orders of the President of the Tax Agency

Order 713 of 12 October 2004 on the approval of the Charter of the rights and obligations of taxpayers during the fiscal inspection.

Orders of the President of the AML/CFT Office

Order 102 of 22.01.2020 regarding the approval of the Norms for the application of the provisions of Law no. 129/2019 for preventing and combating money laundering and terrorist financing, as well as for amending and supplementing some normative acts for the reporting entities supervised and controlled by the National Office for Prevention and Combating Money Laundering.

Decisions of the AML/CFT Office Plenary

Decision of the Plenary of the Office 673/2008 for the approval of the Working Methodology regarding the transmission of cash transaction reports and external transfer reports;
Decision of the Plenary of the Office 2742/2013 on the form and content of the Suspicious Transaction Report, the Cash Transaction Report and the External Transfer Report.

COMING SOON

COMING SOON

◆ ◆ ◆

"Your money is here". Where, exactly? Let's see together. The Budget of Romania is the money bag to which all the Romanian tax residents contribute. In that case, shouldn't we know, in full transparency, where our money goes? Do we really know now what is happening with each penny of our money? Probably not, without transparent instruments. But could we theoretically know, in real-time? Definitely yes, with a tailored platform. Until then, though, the first step is to have the annual financial statements audited and published.

COMING SOON

❖ ❖ ❖

Michael is in love with Amy, but their love is put to the test when he is offered a promising job in a different city. Amy will only be able to join him after one year, when she graduates from her studies. They speak about it at length and are confident everything will be great, but will things change as time passes? Will he still manage to offer Amy the time together they both need?

COMING SOON

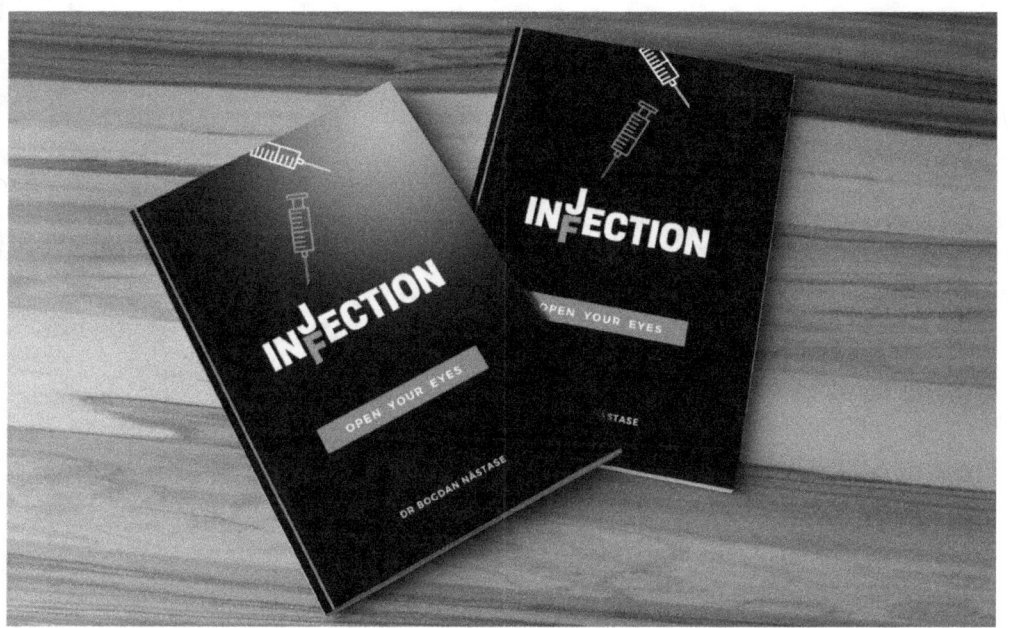

◆ ◆ ◆

Any injection is a gateway for microbes into the organism. This book displays one of the risks we face when entering a medical clinic. The level of risk is raised to an extreme when the injection is performed without consent.

www.ingramcontent.com/pod-product-compliance
Lightning Source LLC
Chambersburg PA
CBHW070632220526
45466CB00001B/158